Cool BrandLeaders

AN INSIGHT INTO BRITAIN'S COOLEST BRANDS 2003

Australia • Britain • China • Czech Republic • Denmark • Egypt • France • Germany • Hong Kong
India • Indonesia • Ireland • Italy • Malaysia • Morocco • The Netherlands • Norway • Philippines
Portugal • Saudi Arabia • Singapore • Spain • Sweden • Thailand • UAE • United States
www.superbrands.org

EDITOR-IN-CHIEF Marcel Knobil

AUTHORS Rebecca Barnes, James Curtis, Helen Jones, Delwyn Swingewood, Mark Tungate

MANAGING EDITOR Angela Pumphrey

EDITORIAL ASSISTANT Emma Selwyn

DESIGNER Verity Belcher, Creative & Commercial Communications

ART DIRECTOR Adam Selwyn, Creative & Commercial Communications

BRAND LIAISON DIRECTOR Annie Richardson

Special thanks to: **Mintel** for providing a considerable amount of market research material.

Other publications from Superbrands in the UK:
Consumer Superbrands ISBN: 0-9541532-1-9
Business Superbrands ISBN: 0-9528153-8-9

For Superbrands publications dedicated to: Australia, China, Czech Republic, Denmark, Egypt, France, Germany, Hong Kong, India, Indonesia, Ireland, Italy, Malaysia, Morocco, The Netherlands, Norway, Philippines, Portugal, Saudi Arabia, Singapore, Spain, Sweden, Thailand, UAE and United States email: brands@superbrands.org or telephone: 0207 267 8899.

To order a copy of Cool BrandLeaders please call 01825 723398

© 2003 Superbrands Ltd

Published by Superbrands Ltd
64 West Yard, Camden Lock Place, London. NW1 8AF

www.superbrands.org/coolbrandleaders

Printed in Italy. ISBN: 0-9541532-4-3

The Independent Authority on Branding

This is the second edition of Cool BrandLeaders and is part of a pioneering and exciting programme that was founded with the aim of paying tribute to the UK's coolest brands.

A dedicated cool judging panel (listed below) has been formulated consisting of eminent individuals who are well qualified to judge which are the nation's coolest brands. Each brand in this book has qualified to be featured based on the ranking of this judging panel.

Through identifying these brands, and providing their case histories, the organisation hopes that people will gain a greater appreciation of the discipline of branding and a greater admiration for the brands themselves.

Beyond this cool branding bible, the Cool BrandLeader programme 2003 encompasses a dedicated Cool BrandLeaders website (www.superbrands.org/coolbrandleaders); Cool BrandLeaders Tribute Event; Cool BrandNoon – an exhibition open to the public; Cool BrandMonth which consists of a series of parties; other events about cool branding, as well as constant appearances by representatives of The Brand Council on TV, radio and in newspapers commenting upon branding.

Cool BrandLeader JUDGES 2003

RALPH ARDILL
Marketing & Strategic Planning Director,
Imagination

DANIEL BARTON
Head of Marketing & Communications,
Diesel Group UK

KAREN BIRCH
Marketing Director, Kangol Ltd

OZWALD BOATENG
Savile Row Tailor & Menswear Designer

SIOBHAN CURTIN
Marketing Manager, Piaggio Ltd

MARCEL KNOBIL
Chairperson,
Cool BrandLeaders Judging Panel

OWEN LEE & GARY ROBINSON
Creative Partners, Farm

RANKIN
Dazed & Confused

MARK RODOL
Chief Executive,
Ministry of Sound

ALEXANDRA SHULMAN
Editor, Vogue

ALON SHULMAN
Chairman, World Famous Group

DON SMITH
Founder, eyestorm

DARREN THOMAS
Managing Director, Cake Group Ltd

Is a nomination as a Cool BrandLeader the highest accolade for a brand? Building a strong brand is complex enough. As we all know, it is all about building in people's minds a belief about your particular product or service – a belief that can only be built through superior performance consistently delivered over time. A cool brand goes further. It must be considered cool to the individual and at the same time observed as cool amongst others. No brand-owning company can determine what is cool. It is an accolade that can only be awarded by the individual – and is all the more valuable for being so. The British Brands Group, as the voice for brands in the UK, is committed to building an environment in which such brands can flourish.

JOHN NOBLE Director, British Brands Group

'Cool BrandLeaders' makes you think about what matters today.

It challenges our conventional thinking about what creates a great brand, and indeed what consumers want from it. 'Cool' makes brands even more relevant to the audience they seek. Cool BrandLeaders connect with consumers, particularly those that set the style agenda. Cool isn't about being flashy and expensive, its about being authentic and real. With the rise of 'cool hunters' and trend forecasters, being cool is a key marketing tool in the search for competitive leadership. However the hardest part is to sustain your coolness, which is evident from the number of changes in this year's list from last year.

The Chartered Institute of Marketing is delighted to endorse Cool BrandLeaders, which has not only independently identified some of the UK's coolest brands, but has also dug deep under the surface to uncover what truly makes them so powerful.

PETER FISK CEO, The Chartered Institute of Marketing

What makes a brand cool? It's all sorts of things that scare the pants off uncool brands. It's cool leaders. It's cool customers. It's cool ideas. It's instinct, inspiration, fearlessness. It's not being scared to be different. It's not relying on research, arse covering, or pandering to the financial institutions. It's doing it, rather than talking about it. It's zigging whilst the others zag. The truth is, cool brands are amazingly easy to create. So long as you're cool.

The Cool BrandLeaders publication brings together insights into many of the brands that have achieved this enviable position and whilst they can not be copied in order to create a cool proposition for your brand they do provide valuable insights to draw upon.

ROBERT CAMPBELL Member of the IPA Creative Forum and
Joint Creative Director of Rainey Kelly Campbell Roalfe/Y&R

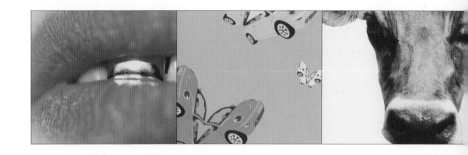

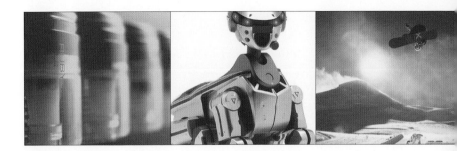

Cool credentials are so critical to numerous brands: recent research by NFO WorldGroup revealed that over half of people are willing to pay more for a brand because it's cool. Yet attaining and maintaining cool status is a phenomenally difficult challenge. The brands that appear in this book have earned the right to do so having been evaluated by many of the most discerning experts in the nation (see over).

They all conform to the following criteria: 'Cool BrandLeaders are brands that have become extremely desirable among many style leaders and influencers. They have a magic about them, signifying that users have an exceptional sense of taste and style.'

An indication of how tough it is to maintain cool status is that out of all the brands that qualified for Cool BrandLeader status last year less than half proved successful on this occasion. It's so difficult to become cool and so easy to lose it.

Achieving cool can occur by accident; staying cool takes considerable flair. Many of the brands on the following pages have managed to skilfully navigate their way through the cool brand landscape for many years. The pages ahead provide illuminating examples of how they have done it.

Flick through and you are confronted by an abundance of: inspirational thinking; audacious creativity; authentic products; radical design; stunning photography; original advertising; and consistent spitting in the face of convention. Enjoy.

MARCEL KNOBIL
Chairperson, Cool BrandLeaders Judging Panel

The nature of cool never changes only the degree of our obsession with it. The more we analyse and try to exploit it the 'warmer' it becomes. There's a law in science that says we can never truly measure anything because the act of observation changes the very thing we are trying to measure. So it is with cool... leave it alone, let it find us and the cooler it will get.

RALPH ARDILL
Marketing & Strategic Planning Director
Imagination

In its more commercial guise and thanks to media obsession with celebrity and product placement, cool has started moving into mainstream consciousness very quickly. For example, if David Beckham has a new haircut, the following day, every Tom, Dick and Harry wants the same cut.

The problem with this of course is that it lasts about as long as milk before it is forgotten and deemed 'so last week'. A more long lasting version is being achieved by avoiding the intoxication of the mainstream media spotlight for as long as possible and relying on word of (relevant) mouth to achieve cool status.

Finally, where once cool could be attached to something less cool (via sponsorship etc) in the hope that some of it will rub off, it is now crystal clear that this just doesn't work unless there is a natural synergy between the brand and the event. In other words, you need to earn it, you just can't buy it off the agency shelf any more.

DANIEL BARTON
Head of Marketing & Communications
Diesel Group UK

It's harder to buy cool these days.
Being cool no longer carries the pressure of having to wear the right brands, following the very latest fashion trends, listening to the right music, knowing the right bands – all achievable, with a certain amount of money, time and effort. A new generation of coolies have emerged, snubbing all that 'cool' previously dictated. Instead, they exude an effortless sense of personal style and individual expression, with a certain irreverence to the world of fashion. Seeking out anything that appeals to them, resulting in an eclectic mixture of tastes from the very new and undiscovered to the institutional. In brand terms, a return to pure, honest product design, quality and reputation has surfaced, with many older, traditional brands now often surprised to find themselves designated cool.
Cool has become indefinable.
It would seem the secret is not to try.
Cool just is.

KAREN BIRCH
Marketing Director
Kangol Ltd

It seems to me that what is 'cool' today has a great deal more to do with individuality and integrity than it used to. Take fashion. Trends have been re-hashed time and time again and yet, in the last few years, people put more thought into how they dress, rather then faithfully following a season's specific trends.

They seem to seek a look that is more a reflection of their own personality. There is an emphasis on HOW people wear their clothes, rather than what they wear, which label they buy or how much it costs. I think this is particularly true in Britain. For me, the coolest thing is someone who is happy with who they are, at ease in their skin and confident enough to follow their beliefs in every area of their life.

OZWALD BOATENG
Savile Row Tailor &
Menswear Designer

A relationship with a brand is very personal and says something about you as a person. Today, people strive to be different, which I think has resulted in cool brands becoming more diverse. People tend to dip in and out of the latest trends in music, fashion, food and drink, the arts etc depending on what the media and celebrities are dictating at the time. An increase in consumer spending has contributed to a more competitive market place, which has led to a decrease in brand loyalty. The key today is to not make it look like you are trying to be cool. A cool brand has to have its own personality and retain its individuality in an ever-changing environment.

It has to retain an air of exclusivity but at the same time appear to be achievable to everyone. A truly cool brand must be able to stand the test of time and maintain its personality and originality so that it appeals to the next generation.

SIOBHAN CURTIN
Marketing Manager
Piaggio Ltd

Read though this book and you will identify a combination of characteristics that tend to reveal themselves in virtually every brand featured: a sense of not trying too hard; freshness and creativity; self-assuredness; and authenticity.

If the nature of cool is changing, it is not that these characteristics have radically altered over recent years, but the 'authenticity' volume is being turned up. People are tired of bullshit whether it be delivered by the media, politicians, or brands. There has been a shift from superficiality and pretentiousness to a demand for integrity and substance.

The brands on the following pages might have supreme images but they also deliver and often do so immaculately.

MARCEL KNOBIL
Chairperson
Cool BrandLeaders Judging Panel

The nature of cool is not changing. The one thing about being cool is you remain true to who you are and follow your beliefs. If people like what you're doing, especially young people then the chances are you'll be cool.

OWEN LEE &
GARY ROBINSON
Creative Partners
Farm

The nature of cool, at least of genuine, unmanufactured cool, never changes. Cool is now, always has been and always will be a function of individualism and originality of attitude, thought and expression. It's not something you can set out to be, it's only something that you can observe in others. How cool is manifested and deemed by others is always changing. In the world of marketing where cool is bought and sold, the change seems to be the sheer quantity of people who are now employed solely to make a label, drink, t-shirt or personality cool. The change seems to be in the fact that people genuinely feel that 'cool' is a quality they can quantify, package and ultimately sell. It's too self-conscious a process and to be honest, sometimes it makes me feel a bit ill. Having said that, any briefs for commercial projects, send 'em over!!!

RANKIN
Dazed & Confused

You can find cool anywhere. But the trick is never to preach it once you've found it. Cool as an underground phenomenon is increasingly a myth. The whole idea of 'underground' has been blown out of the water by mass access to music, fashion, style, art and, clubs, as all these things have been irreversibly co-opted by mainstream brands before they have a chance to breathe. Is this such a bad thing? Cool is as likely to be found on day-time TV as it might in a New York loft. Anyone can do cool-by-numbers – wear the right trainers, listen to the right music – in other words, 'cool' is now about conformity. Real cool is about not being scared to take risks, standing out on a limb, sticking up for what you care about and doing it all with a smile on your face.

MARK RODOL
Chief Executive
Ministry of Sound

It's hard to define anything about 'cool' as the very notion of cool itself, is somewhat uncool at the moment. Individuality is what everybody is keen on – whether that be a bespoke handbag or a tailor-made trek in the Himalayas. That still means that there are some brands that people admire more than others but they tend to have defined themselves by their differences rather than their similarities. The growth of mass-market cool is increasingly found among the very young – even pre teen – rather than the adults with the greater spending power.

ALEXANDRA SHULMAN
Editor
Vogue

Cool is an unusual concept. It fuses perception with reality and while being an essential part of many peoples day is irrelevant to many. For some it is all about acceptance while for the 'style leaders' it is about being different. You constantly hear that cool is evolving – but from what and into what?

However, what is certain is that the values surrounding 'cool' are an instrumental part in shaping modern youth culture and the wider world that surrounds it. I would just simply say; "Cool Is!"

ALON SHULMAN
Chairman
World Famous Group

Entering the world of cool is like walking through an art gallery and seeking out the true masterpieces. Some are pretty obvious while others appeal on a more personal level. Cool brands stir the senses and provoke discussion in the way a piece of art awakens ones emotions.

However, 'cool' is now oozing into every corner of our lives – from fashion to restaurants, cars to drinks. We are bombarded with 'coolness' and so are increasingly wary of what cool is.

Brands therefore need to work hard at it, whilst making it seem effortless, to ensure that they respect their own DNA, build on it and evolve around it. Layers of superficiality are so easily peeled away that brands that lack honest, pioneering and true qualities are mocked or lost somewhere in the mass market.

True Cool BrandLeaders, like great artists, will be remembered in centuries to come for shocking, delighting, intriguing and luring us towards them as well as evoking feelings of pride and respect for their individuality.

DON SMITH
Founder
eyestorm

Cool is now about coming from reality rather than spin. I don't mean reality TV shows I mean from truth, honesty, and good old-fashioned quality. Nowadays people are too smart to be hood-winked by fancy packaging and glossy ads; if it's a crap product, it remains crap – you can't polish it.

DARREN THOMAS
Managing Director
Cake Group Ltd

Agent Provocateur

Known for revolutionising the lingerie market, Agent Provocateur has been designing seductive lingerie for students, secretaries, strippers and celebrities alike since 1994.

Owners Joseph Corre and Serena Rees' first store in London's Soho featured a sexy boudoir interior and stylish assistants in uniforms designed by Vivienne Westwood. Based around the concept of seduction and the way a garment feels as well as looks, the aim was to create high-quality lingerie to stimulate, enchant and arouse both wearers and their partners.

Now known the world over for their erotic designs, Agent Provocateur has become a phenomenal success with the opening of additional stores, a thriving mail-order catalogue business and a cutting-edge website.

From searching for unknowns to front the range, to utilising 'live' shop windows and organising private cinema screenings, Corre and Rees have always put a distinctive spin on marketing, which has earned them vital column inches in the national and international press, including Vogue, The Sunday Times, Playboy, Financial Times and The Face.

In the late 1990s Agent Provocateur launched the Salon Rose range in partnership with Marks & Spencer. This took the brand to high streets throughout the UK, whilst adding a bit of spice to the Marks & Spencer's lingerie department.

In 2002 Agent Provocateur's notorious cinema advertising campaign featuring Kylie Minogue undressing in a slow, sexy way ensured that the website – which won the BIMA award for best retail website the same year – received over 400,000 hits in one month.

It isn't surprising that Agent Provocateur has already gone down in fashion history – in 1997 a selection of garments were included in the V&A's permanent collection, while in 2000, the company contributed to the Inside Out exhibition at London's Design Museum, which travelled to all corners of the world.

The first overseas store was opened in Los Angeles in October 2001, with the launch attracting a host of A-list celebrities. That year, the FiFi award for Best New Fragrance was also clinched, along with a special award for Creative Imagery.

In July 2002 a third London store opened at The Royal Exchange in the city's financial district, while October saw the first Agent Provocateur in-store boutique open in uptown New York's Henri Bendel, finally bringing Sex to the City and satisfying New Yorker's demands for saucy undies.

Following the success of the New York outlet, November 2002 saw Agent Provocateur opening its largest store to-date in downtown SoHo's Mercer Street. With a sophisticated boudoir feel, the 1,200 square foot flagship store features lace-print wallpaper, chandeliers, mirrored display tables and antique furniture.

Hotel Agent Provocateur, a postcard size catalogue was launched at the end of the year. Complete with a Do Not Disturb sign and a menu full of scantily dressed fantasies, it is set to become a collector's item.

In celebration of their 40th anniversary tour, The Rolling Stones commissioned the brand to design a seriously sexy collection – all-over prints of the iconic tongue logo, leopard print trimmed with lace and sexy tassel sets left little to the imagination, and were launched at the 40 Licks fashion show in LA. Before the event Corre and Rees said, "We love Rock-n-Roll girls and who better to work with on such a project than the Rolling Stones. These girls are going to get their rocks off on Sunday night."

In July 2003 Agent Provocateur opened a 1,000 square foot in-store boutique in Selfridges London. Yet more fantasies will be aided with another boutique, which is due to open in Selfridges Birmingham in autumn 2003.

agentprovocateur.com

ALEXANDER
MCQUEEN

Theatrical, dramatic and at the
pinnacle of British fashion design

Alexander McQueen is the undisputed 'bad boy'
of British fashion, and one of the most successful
designers in the world. He is often cited by other
designers as being an inspiration to the rest of
the fashion world.

It has been an incredible rise for the East End
son of a taxi-driver, who left school at the age
of sixteen to his position now aged 34, as the
three-times winner of 'British Designer of the
Year'. Indeed, when he first won this award in
1996 he was one of the youngest designers ever
to do so. McQueen continues to be award
winning – in June 2003 the Council of Fashion
Designers of America presented him with the
accolade of 'International Designer of the Year'.

McQueen has worked with Koji Tatsuno as
well as the French fashion house Givenchy as the
chief designer. He has also become known outside
fashion circles as a celebrity in his own right.

McQueen's road to earning his reputation
as a 'master cutter' began when he became an
apprentice at Gieves and Hawkes tailors in

Saville Row. Legend has it, that he scrawled
'McQueen was here' inside the lining of a jacket
made for the Prince of Wales. His colourful
career has also seen him at the famous theatrical
costumiers Angels and Bermans. The combination
of these experiences allowed McQueen to
master six methods of pattern cutting, from the
melodramatic sixteenth century to the brutally
sharp tailoring that has become his signature.

Now, the likes of Madonna, Kate Moss, The
Rolling Stones, David Bowie and Liv Tyler are

amongst his client list, and his wildly theatrical fashion shows such as 'The Overlook' and 'Eye' have captured worldwide attention and underlined London's reputation as a global capital of style.

McQueen's creations have inspired several high street trends, including his low-cut 'bumster' trousers which first hit the catwalk in 1992. Typically blending drama, controversy and simple street style, some of his clothes are deliberately shocking show-stoppers, but others are eminently wearable. Tweed, satin and leather skirt-suits, jackets with hoods and billowing sleeves, knitted tank tops and trousers with curved hems can all be found in his portfolio.

In December 2000 the Gucci Group acquired 51% of the Alexander McQueen label, with McQueen serving as creative director. This helped to propel Alexander McQueen onto an even bigger stage, with the opening of stores worldwide and expansion into areas such as eyewear and perfume – his first fragrance, Kingdom, launched in the UK in spring 2003.

alexandermcqueen.com

In addition to having his collections sold in the finest fashion stores, in July 2002, Alexander McQueen opened his first store in New York, which was followed by the UK flagship store, which opened in London's Old Bond Street in March 2003. Furthermore a store is due to open in Milan in July 2003 with plans also underway for stores in Paris and Los Angeles.

The Alexander McQueen brand continues to be bestowed great acclaim but McQueen's place in fashion history has already been firmly sealed.

Asahi
ASAHI BEER

> Clean, crisp, clear and oozing with Japanese style

Forget pottery and paper folding – Asahi, pronounced 'a-sa-hee' is one of Japan's oldest premium lagers. The beer was Japan's first bottled draft beer and was established 114 years ago. It is currently Japan's biggest beer brand, but has also travelled well and is now the world's sixth biggest beer brand (Source: Impact 2001).

The name Asahi means 'Rising Sun' and the brand lies at the core of cutting edge Japanese style. It is the beer of choice for young, style conscious, socially nocturnal creatures, who appreciate its clean, crisp flavour with a hint of citrus and contemporary, slightly elitist image.

Not content with launching the nation's first canned beer way back in 1958, in the late 1980s, Asahi breweries began to study the changes that were taking place in Japanese food culture – by understanding what people ate, they hoped to create the finest-tasting beverages to complement those foods.

The result was Asahi Super Dry, which was launched in 1987. With more and more bars carrying imported premium beers and indeed the favourable reception they received amongst drinkers, particularly in London, sales of Asahi Super Dry increased steadily since its introduction.

In order to ensure that the Asahi sold in Europe is as fresh as that in its native Japan, the brand has been brewed in Prague since 2000. Asahi naturally ensures that the beer is brewed to the same specification as it is in

Master the art
of pronunciation.
Ah-Sah-Hee

PURE BEER JAPAN STYLE
Japan's No.1 Beer www.asahibeer.co.uk

Be patient my son
he'll buy another
round eventually

PURE BEER JAPAN STYLE
Japan's No.1 Beer www.asahibeer.co.uk

Japan. Ingredients include the finest quality water, malt, maize, hops and rice.

Over the years, Asahi has won many industry awards and accolades, more recently the 1999 and 2000 Award of Excellence for Advanced Business Facilities and the Second Grand Prize for Ozone Layer Preservation, both from the Nihon Keizai Shimbun, and the Minister of Environment Award from the Japan Industrial Journal.

In line with the current warmth towards Japanese style, which envelops the bar and restaurant sector, trendier establishments all over the country have been recognising Asahi. It can be found in urban cool bars, clubs, hotels and restaurants including Alphabet, China White, Lab, Zuma and the Sanderson, along with more traditional Japanese venues.

Keen to get into the well-groomed hands of movers and shakers at the best launches and parties, recent Asahi sponsorship events have included London Film Festival, Kyoto Jazz Massive's UK Tour, the Nordoff-Robbins World DJ Day launch party, numerous London Fashion Week events and Selfridge's Tokyo Life campaign.

Asahi also supports art installations, cult films and fashion parties, as well as advertising in edgy fashion and lifestyle publications, while branded rickshaws also wind their way through the crowded streets of central London.

The brand is also undertaking its biggest-ever marketing campaign in 2003 with a two month long advertising campaign with four executions that draw on the brand's Japanese heritage. It was launched on the London Underground, Glasgow and Manchester Metrolinks and the Newcastle Metro – all breeding grounds for the brand's urban and cosmopolitan potential followers.

asahibeer.co.uk

Audi

Audi has become a byword for intelligent, sophisticated, German technology. But it's also about an emotional response to progress, not just technology for technology's sake.

The brand began life when August Horch, a pioneering engineer with a reputation for being able to solve complex problems, set up a company in 1901. By 1901 he had created his first automobile and the following year he became convinced of the need to use light weight alloys to reduce mass – this same principal was used in the first Audi A8, and in the latest manifestation of the A8, where the body is around 50% lighter than if it were made of steel.

In 1909 August Horch, whose surname means listen in German, started a new company called Audi, which also translates as listen in Latin. He began entering his cars into motor sport events and won a string of prizes. It's a tradition that continues to this day. Audi dominated British Touring Cars with the A4 in the 1990s and has won the Le Mans 24 hour race for three years running.

In the 1980s, its advertising slogan Vorsprung durch Technik – meaning progress through technology – entered the English language and even made its way into the song Parklife by Blur. It's a phrase that sums up not only Audi's technical excellence but also its emotional attitude to design which reached its zenith in the shape of the Audi TT.

Audi has long recognised that consumers don't buy cars for purely rational reasons. It wanted to appeal to their emotional side so in 1999 the unmistakeable Audi TT was launched to great acclaim. It has become the epitome of 'cool' and a design classic. It is also hailed as one of the few cars that has changed little from concept stage to final production. The designers apparently listened to Jimmy Hendrix for inspiration during the creative process.

Audi describes it as clarity and form combined with advanced technology. Emotion not indifference. It is designed for people with passion – creative individuals with a desire for the extraordinary. But, creatively minded or not, its difficult not to appreciate its low, sleek, sexy and sporty silhouette licking the road.

Audi also appeals to the emotions with its other marques. The Audi A4 FSI, for example, appeared in a remarkable TV commercial in 2003 which features huge fish swimming around urban streets gasping for breath and guzzling fuel while the A4 glides effortlessly through them.

The new Audi A8, which was launched in May 2003, also focuses on innovation. It is described by the company as a luxury saloon with the advanced technology one would expect from Audi with the spirit of a sports car. The supporting advertising campaign focuses on Audi's innovative history – it was the first to perform systematic crash tests, the first to break the 400kph land speed record and the first to introduce a permanent four wheel drive rally car.

And as part of the company's commitment to design it has set up the Audi Design Foundation to encourage and support people to bring innovative designs to fruition. To date it has awarded over half a million pounds to young designers to help them bring their ideas to life.

audi.co.uk

BANG & OLUFSEN B&O

Courage to constantly question the
ordinary in search of surprising,
long lasting experiences

Design drives Bang & Olufsen. The brand epitomises the
attributes of good design: durability, unity, integrity and
inevitability. Innovation and intelligent ideas that defy
expectations are part of the brand's DNA.

The two people who were responsible for bringing this
concept alive are Peter Bang and Svend Olufsen. This duo
literally redefined radio by successfully marrying form and
function. The first set rolled off the production line at their
little factory in northern Denmark in 1925. These young
engineers not only produced something that transformed
the radio from a utilitarian device into a status symbol but
on the technological front were acoustically light years ahead
of anything else on the market. A radio that sounded natural.

The 1920s and 1930s may have been the radio decades
but the company was also in the vanguard of change during
the 1950s and 1960s. When transistors revolutionised the
industry the company completely redesigned the vocabulary
of audio equipment. In 1991 the brand broke new ground
with the BeoSystem 2500, the first hi-fi unit to stand tall
amongst the flat rack systems of its day.

The brand's contribution to design and technology through its hi-fi systems, tape recorders, televisions and of course radios, is recognised by no less an institution than New York's Museum of Modern Art which boasts 21 B&O products in its permanent design collection.

Bang & Olufsen has an annual turnover of around $1 billion but remains a small independent company giving it the freedom to develop products in its own time. Five-strong teams of designers, engineers and 'consumer demand forecasters' work in what the company calls 'Idea Land' to define products up to seven years in advance. Only a fraction of these ideas actually go into production as the technology must always be completely correct.

Its latest product, the BeoLab 5 loudspeaker gives listeners the same sound quality wherever they are in a room. At the touch of a button the speaker analyses a room's dimensions then calibrates itself to reflect the acoustic environment. The product is the result of twenty years of research not only in speaker technology but how the human ear perceives sound. The sound reproduction delivered by the system is so pure that the human ear never tires.

The BeoLab 5, like many other B&O systems is startling for its revolutionary design and state of the art-technology. But the company doesn't believe in technology for technology's sake. A golden rule for B&O designers is that their products should make someone smile when they see it. A typical Bang & Olufsen product communicates with the customers. It should say; "Please come and use me. Please come and enjoy me".

Bang & Olufsen's extension into non-core activities such as its medical and business to business division embody the brand's values. Unlike traditional industrial audio-visual, telecommunications and medical components, Bang & Olufsen products are engineered not only for performance but to create a total aesthetic experience. Designing products that are not only exceptionally functional but also aesthetically pleasing, requires a strong commitment to engineering and engineering technologies.

The B&O trademark, designed by an apprentice in 1932 and still in use today, symbolises the elegant simplicity reflected in all the company's products. This philosophy is extended to the brand's uncluttered advertising which reflects the attitude of its style conscious consumers and mirrors design elements on the B&O website, in its stores and throughout everything else it touches.

bang-olufsen.com

REG. TM.

BECK'S

An international beer with a taste for contemporary art

The Chapman Brothers 2003

An iconic green bottle, its long neck wrapped in silver and an oval red and white label is distinctively Beck's.

The brand is a German premium pilsner beer which is available in 120 countries around the world. Today an excess of 2,000 million bottles of Beck's are drunk every year in the UK alone, where the brand has been present since 1984.

Beck's is brewed in strict accordance with the 'Reinheitsgebot' a German purity law of 1516, which means that only barley malt, hops, yeast and water can be used in the brewing process.

As early as the mid 1920s over 250,000 hectolitres of Beck's were being sold around the world annually. At this time there was hardly a luxury ship cruising the world's oceans or a grand hotel in south east Asia which didn't stock the brand.

When Beck's was first brought to the UK, it was initially only available in the most influential bars and at the hippest parties. Through word of mouth the brand's reputation grew. The perception of the brand as one for discerning drinkers was enhanced further by its decision to focus on sponsoring British contemporary art.

Beck's was directly involved in the emergence of what became known as 'Brit Art'. Its sponsorship programme started with the major 'German Art of the 20th Century' exhibition. Since then, Beck's has been involved in a series of major public art commissions. Two works by Rachel Whiteread, have been ranked amongst the most significant contemporary art commissions ever. Beck's other commissions have included pieces by the likes of Tony Oursler and Douglas Gordon.

Beck's continues to sponsor gallery openings by supplying drink. From high profile shows, such as Hirst's seminal one-man show at White Cube in 1995, where snooty St. James' in London is brought to a standstill by revellers, celebs, art students and drag queens clutching bottles of Beck's to other much smaller exhibitions.

Beck's Futures (www.becksfutures.co.uk) is the richest prize in British Contemporary Art, developed with the support of the Institute of Contemporary Art it recognises the work of emerging artists practicing in the UK. First awarded in 1999 Beck's Futures has rapidly established itself as an important barometer of what is happening at the grassroots of new British Art. Often challenging, sometimes controversial Beck's Futures reflects the brand's willingness to engage in the debate about the nature of art and its relationship to business.

One of the most innovative ideas from Beck's has been the famous limited edition artist's bottles. There have been 23 bottles since the first, which was created by Gilbert and George. They are usually released to coincide with a major show or artistic milestone. Other contributors have included Damien Hirst, Tracey Emin, Jeff Koons, Sam Taylor-Wood to name but a few. In 2003 two designs were created by the Chapman Brothers, their involvement again demonstrates that Beck's has supported some of the most important and influential artists of the modern era. Beck's limited edition artists bottles have become highly collectable works of art often fetching hundreds of pounds at auction with Tate Modern being one of the few institutions to possess a full set.

Beck's recent advertising campaign 'the bottle reveals the drinker' has been its most successful yet. It centred on the brand's main asset – the bottle. Beck's found that drinkers have a tendency to play with Beck's labels, whether it be scratching off the foil at the top, peeling the label off the front, or changing its appearance in some other way. It was also found that groups of friends like to play the part of amateur psychologist – analysing each other on the basis of what they've done to their label. Reflecting this, the Beck's print ads show bottles that have been tampered with which reveal something about the drinker.

www.becks.co.uk

becks.co.uk

NUNC EST BIBENDUM

Walking into the building that was established as the UK head quarters of the Michelin Tyre Company in 1911, you know instantly that Bibendum is no ordinary restaurant. Acclaimed designer and restaurateur Sir Terence Conran and famed publisher, Lord Hamlyn, acquired the famous building in 1985 and opened the restaurant in 1987. Bibendum has since become established as one of London's most elegant and renowned eateries.

The name Bibendum comes from the previous occupants of the building and one of its early marketing campaigns that dates back to 1898. A series of posters were produced which showed a character made from tyres drinking nails and broken bottles and claiming 'Nunc est Bibendum' – Latin for 'Now is the time to drink' – to emphasise that Michelin tyres could 'swallow' obstacles without creating punctures. The character in the ad, which has represented Michelin ever since, became know as Bibendum – more commonly dubbed the Michelin Man. Bibendum the restaurant has now become and icon in its own right, with the location, ambience, design, food and wine all combining to create a world-class venue.

The masterly design touches of Conran were developed over a two-year period during which the building was restored and the concept developed. Extensive research into the Michelin archives helped Conran achieve a beautiful retro-feel, using the tyre company's heritage to create a distinctive ambience.

Distinctive cuisine in artfully cultivated surroundings

Bibendum's corpulent profile is evident in the designs of the restaurant's famous stained glass windows, which bathe the graceful, high-ceilinged main dining room in effervescent light. Street plans of French gastronomic cities are also etched into the windows. Bright blue bucket chairs (all of the furniture was designed by Sir Terence, while his son Jasper styled the chair covers) sit on lush pistachio coloured carpets and a collection of French artworks add to the dining area's easy style. Conran described the interior as "ebullient".

When it opened, Bibendum was hailed as leading the way in the British culinary revolution, representing all that was fresh and innovative in restaurant design, concept and food. And let's not forget the food. Head chef Matthew Harris (he's been there since 1989) oversees a menu boasting the best of British combined with old-fashioned French bistro food. Poached sea-bass with Champagne sauce and oysters, sit alongside crab vinaigrette with herbs and scallops saute provencal. Harris is especially fond of game and offal, giving diners the chance to savour warm calves with cucumber and chervil vinaigrette.

There is also an Oyster Bar, which serves oysters, caviar and other seafood in a relaxed setting, while the recently launched Bibendum Café, offers a variety of rolls, organic breads, soups, pastries and cakes. Accentuating the feel of easy continental style, the Citroen Camionette (the Crustacea Van) spills outside and sells a seasonal selection of fresh fish and seafood, including lobster, crab, salmon and oysters.

It is the style and quality that Bibendum exudes which has attracted wide acclaim. When it launched, the critics were swept away, with the Evening Standard's Fay Maschler stating that Bibendum "has the somewhat breathless feeling of visions given substance". A true reflection of a style leader is its ability to stay at the front, and Bibendum continues to set the pace. The Evening Standard recently declared it is "still a world-class restaurant, with "careful, beautiful design" and The Good Food Guide 2003 calls it a "cherished place...with food to gladden the heart".

bibendum.co.uk

There is an element of mystery to Bombay Sapphire. It's a brand which carries the classic hallmarks of quality and heritage, yet oozes contemporary style. A bottle of Bombay Sapphire is an elegant design accessory – whether it's in cocktail bars around the world or in the home – but just as importantly, it tastes sublime.

Bombay Sapphire has certainly changed the way we think about gin. Crafted from 100% Scottish grain spirit, Bombay Sapphire is infused with the delicate aromas of no less than ten botanical flavourings – most gins are produced using between four and six, of which juniper is the most dominant.

Little expense is spared in sourcing the finest quality ingredients from around the world. These include juniper berries from Italy, coriander from Morocco, almonds and lemon peel from Spain, liquorice from China and grains of paradise from West Africa. As a result, Bombay Sapphire has a complexity and subtlety of flavour which is beyond juniper-fuelled gins and makes it the spirit of choice for many discerning gin drinkers.

The brand attracts such a passionate following that it has established its cool credentials without taking a traditional advertising route. Instead, young, style-conscious individuals are discovering for themselves the alluring appeal of Bombay Sapphire and are spreading the word.

A design icon with its own distinctive taste

In the hottest cocktail bars, Bombay Sapphire is the first choice of many of the world's top mixologists. Based on a secret recipe which dates back to 1761, Bombay Sapphire's distinctive taste is unexpectedly clean, crisp and yet subtle, making it an ideal cocktail ingredient. Its versatility means that it not only creates impressive gin cocktails, but can improve on cocktails which are traditionally vodka-based – like the Cosmopolitan or the Bloody Mary.

Bombay Sapphire is not only known for its distinctive flavour – its striking, translucent blue glass bottle is a style icon. It successfully combines classic elements with a contemporary edge. It is fitting then that Bombay Sapphire is a strong supporter of international design. The Bombay Sapphire Foundation was established in 2001 to support and reward excellence in the use of glass for contemporary living. Foundation members include prominent designers such as Marc Newson, Nicole Farhi, Thomas Heatherwick, Ron Arad and Tom Dixon. Central to the Foundation's support for design is The Bombay Sapphire Prize, the world's biggest annual glass design award which was launched in 2002. The Bombay Sapphire Prize rewards innovation and excellence in the use of glass and is open to international designers, architects and artists. Short-listed entries are showcased in a major exhibition – The Bombay Sapphire Blue Room – which tours the UK each year.

The brand has a permanent presence at Vinopolis on London's Bankside with The Bombay Sapphire Experience. This offers visitors the opportunity to uncover some of the secrets of this intriguing brand. Each of the ten botanicals that go into the making of the drink can be touched and tasted. One can also learn more about the vapour infusion process, which passes their flavours on to the spirit in the bottle. There is also a Bombay Sapphire bar, where the glowing blue décor mirrors that of the distinctive bottle. The brand's own mixologist prepares and serves the drinks, and, one could say, acts as a benchmark for what a Bombay Sapphire cocktail should really taste like.

BOMBAY SAPPHIRE is a registered trademark.

bombaysapphire.com

BRITISH AIRWAYS

London eye

The British Airways London Eye has quickly
become one of Britain's most famous landmarks.
It instils quiet pride and passion in its citizens and
awe and amazement in all visitors. As well as
providing spectacular views it also animates the
skyline, gives a whole new perspective on the city
and has helped to inject new life into London's
South Bank.

An inspiring, visionary and
genuinely unique structure initiated
by the best of British architecture,
innovation and engineering

But it almost didn't get off the drawing board.
The Eye was designed on the kitchen table of
London architects David Marks and Julia Barfield
as an entry for a competition to create a
structure to celebrate the Millennium.

The competition was eventually abandoned
but Marks and Barfield knew they had a project
worth pursuing – the biggest observation wheel
in the world. With favourable coverage from the
London Evening Standard and support from the
public, the plans reached the attention of British
Airways who decided to form a partnership
with the architects and provide the loans to
get the project started.

The ingredients of the wheel are simple, says Barfield – a universal desire to see the earth and cities from a great height and the natural human fascination with scale, daring structure fused with beauty.

It's also a tremendous feat of engineering. Experts from across Europe were involved in its manufacture and the population of an entire Alpine village tested and re-tested the embarkation process on a mocked up boarding platform.

Shipping the various components to London was a complicated business and delivery had to be carefully timed with the tides so that the largest parts could get under the city's bridges safely. Southwark Bridge was the tightest squeeze with clearance of only 40 centimetres.

In a short time, the London Eye has become a symbol of modern Britain and is now the capital's number one visitor attraction. It has won a large number of architecture, design, tourism and people's choice awards and part of its success has been the careful positioning, design and management of the brand.

Innovative themed events such as opening until midnight to celebrate the Queen's Golden Jubilee, ice sculptures at Christmas, and joint promotions with local restaurants and art galleries, keep visitors flooding in. The London Eye is also a popular corporate entertainment venue and has become a setting for parties, events, product launches, and even weddings, with couples tying the knot whilst in 'flight' above the capital.

Whatever visitors' motivation – to celebrate a special occasion; to see London as they've never seen it before; or for the sheer thrill of travelling 135 metres in the sky, they keep on coming. Perhaps it's because it's a remarkable piece of engineering, and an outstanding landmark, or simply because of its graceful beauty.

ba-londoneye.com

In 1977, Jake Burton founded Burton Snowboards, the world's first snowboarding factory. Jake has dedicated the past 26 years of his life to snowboarding and is Burton's most avid product tester – he strives to snowboard over 100 days per year. Through the years, Jake has played a vital role in transitioning snowboarding from a backyard hobby to a world-class sport.

Headquartered in Burlington, Vermont in the US with offices in Innsbruck, Austria and Tokyo, Japan, Burton has led the snowboard industry for 26 years. Burton also supports a family of companies that includes Gravis Footwear and Anon Optics.

Snowboarding made its debut as an Olympic sport in 1998, with several riders competing on Burton boards. At the 2002 Olympic Games 23 athletes from thirteen different nations represented Burton Snowboards. The two Olympic Halfpipe Gold Medalists Ross Powers and Kelly Clark are both Burton riders as well as Chris Klug, the Bronze Medalist in Parallel Giant Slalom.

In addition to Olympic athletes, Burton sponsors more than 250 snowboarders worldwide with different levels of sponsorship. The top level of sponsorship is Burton's Global Team, which consists of sixteen riders – the best in the world. Burton fully supports these riders, promoting them and including them in marketing initiatives and product development. By supporting a Global Team of the world's top riders, Burton Snowboards has fuelled the growth of snowboarding worldwide. The team also drives the development process at Burton. Pro riders work closely with the Burton technical team

burton.com

and graphic designers to drive innovation in the product development process and test products on the slopes. The result is products that are created for riders, by riders with the perfect blend of technology, artistic design and rider-driven input.

Rider-driven development is key at Burton, but so is innovation and progression. So Burton has pursued partnerships with other progressive companies like Apple Computers to push their products to the next level. In the winter of 2003 Burton and Apple introduced The Burton AMP Jacket, the world's first electronic jacket with an integrated iPod control system. The jacket demonstrates Burton's leadership in style and technical innovations.

Heavy involvement in snowboarding events is also a trademark of Burton. Through successful events like the Burton European Open and the Burton World Tour, Burton actively spreads the word about snowboarding around the world. The Burton European Open is a leading snowboard contest in Europe, broadcasted on main TV channels such as the BBC and Eurosport. The World Tour brings Burton pro riders and the new Burton promo video to cities around Europe, North America and Japan attracting enormous crowds at every stop.

Burton also works at a grass roots level and has developed successful programs like Learn to Ride (LTR) and The Chill Foundation. The LTR program and products are specifically designed to facilitate and accelerate learning so beginner snowboarders have the best learning experience possible. Founded in 1995, the Chill Foundation is a North American intervention programme for disadvantaged inner-city kids. Chill takes underprivileged and at-risk kids snowboarding once a week for six weeks and provides them with everything they need for the experience: lift tickets, instruction, bus transportation and head-to-toe gear.

When it's all said and done, everything Burton Snowboards does orbits around riders. The product development process begins, ends and begins again with riders. Burton never stops innovating and creating. And they never stop listening to snowboarders.

Chloé

Lauded by the fashion press and favoured by celebrities, the house of Chloé has been designing chic,
feminine style since the 1950s. 2003 saw the brand's 50th year in fashion and the glittering anniversary
party was held at the site of the label's first fashion show – Café de Flore in Paris.

   Chloé was founded in 1952 by the elegant Egyptian Gaby Aghion, along with business partner,
Jacques Lenoir. They showcased their first collection four years later at the famous Parisian café
– one of their favourite haunts. Instead of naming the brand after herself, Gaby chose a friend's name,
Chloé, for its warm, feminine appeal. She thought that her own name sounded like the name of
a fortune-teller. The colour of the brand's original logo was inspired by the sunset pink and sand
hues of the Egyptian desert.

   In the 1960s, Chloé spawned a clutch of new, young talents who went on to define the Paris
ready-to-wear movement, 'Le Style'. Karl Lagerfeld became the house's head designer, taking Chloé
to new status as one of the most iconic brands of the time, and A-list celebrities including Brigitte
Bardot, Jackie Kennedy and Grace Kelly flocked to the boutique in Paris's seventh arrondissment
in search of luxurious daywear which when on to define the look of a generation. Legend has it that
Christina Onassis once ordered 36 silk blouses in one visit.

chloe.com

The first to make dresses in jersey cloth (a fabric usually reserved for sweaters), Chloé's signature style was kept fresh and cutting-edge throughout the 1970s by a team of talented designers including Martine Sitbon. 1974 also saw the birth of Chloé perfume – created by cosmetics brand Elizabeth Arden following a commission by Gaby Aghion, this heady, flowery scent was one of the firsts in the ready-to-wear business and a huge success.

After the brand was bought by the Swiss-based luxury goods conglomerate Richemont Group in 1985, its global reputation grew while Martine Sitbon continued to infuse the label with an original blend of femininity and strict chic until Karl Lagerfeld returned as designer in the early 1990s.

In 1997, Stella McCartney reinvented Chloé once more, giving the label a cool, rock and roll edge and reviving vintage lingerie, tailoring and signature low-rider trousers that were worn by her celebrity friends and fashionable young women alike, propelling the house to dizzy new heights of success.

Meanwhile, the must-have accessory at the time became the label's heart-shaped sunglasses with diamond heart engravings, which spawned imitations on high-streets up and down the country.

Since 2001, Chloé's new creative director and fashion maverick, Phoebe Philo, who worked closely alongside Stella McCartney for fours years, has continued the legacy of luxurious pret-a-porter, while infusing the label with her own distinctive style – effortlessly sexy daywear drapes in long, fluid lines, while distinctly modern diaphanous tops skim the shoulders for evening, and are loved by stars including Cameron Diaz and Kate Hudson.

With the unveiling of a new flagship store in London in 2002 also under her belt, Phoebe's next mission is to develop the brand even further with new categories of merchandise, including accessories and swimwear, along with the continued expansion of the already successful diffusion line, See by Chloé.

"You can be watching TV and see Coca-Cola and you can know that the President drinks Coke, Liz Taylor drinks Coke, and just think, you can drink Coke too. A Coke is a Coke and no amount of money can get you a better Coke than the one the bum on the corner is drinking…Liz Taylor knows it, the President knows it, the bum knows it and you know it."
Andy Warhol, 1975.

Coca-Cola is one of the oldest brands in this book, yet still remains as relevant today as ever.

The secret formula runs much deeper than the Coca-Cola recipe stored in a bank vault in Atlanta, Georgia. The brand has an extremely strong heritage and yet through a combination of progressive innovation and leading edge marketing is firmly embedded in modern life.

Over the years Coca-Cola advertising has certainly had an impact on society. The first TV ad to be shown globally was the iconic 1979 'I'd like to buy the world a Coke', which featured young kids from around the world. Many years earlier the world took to its heart the brand's 1930s image of an old man in a red suit – an image we all recognise today as Father Christmas.

A truly iconic brand for all time

Coca-Cola has a long history of supporting sport – in Great Britain its associations go back over 30 years. The brand sponsors major events that unite millions of people such as the Olympic Games and the FIFA World Cup right down to local community and grass roots tournaments including the English Schools Cup and the Scottish Schools Football Association 'Coca-Cola 7s'. In 1996 Coca-Coca Great Britain challenged the then widespread way of advertising to a football audience and turned the camera on the fans themselves. The classic and memorable 'Eat Football, Sleep Football,

Drink Coca-Cola' campaign was created. FIFA World Cup 2002 saw the latest 'Eat, Sleep, Drink' ad with the appearance of a new animated three legged football hero Leggsy. A campaign full of local insights, Leggsy's two left feet reflected England's dearth of left footed players.

The original Coca-Cola glass bottle is a timeless design classic. It was created to be instantly recognisable – even in the dark or when broken. Inspirational to designers and artists like Andy Warhol, the bottle maintains its contemporary relevance as the classic combination of form and function.

So how does the world's most famous brand continue to innovate and surprise consumers in the twenty first century? What continues to make the brand so relevant is its ability to tap into consumers' passions and lifestyles in a way that no other brand can.

In Great Britain Coca-Cola maintains its strong relevance with youth most recently through its active interest in music. The recent 'TXT for Music' promotion got to grips with our growing passion for texting and gave the nation the first chance to text, collect and open a virtual 'account' saving music credits from special cans and bottles which could be swapped for a selection of CDs and access to musical experiences.

Coca-Cola has established strong links with the world of design. The Coca-Cola Original Glass Bottle Lifestyle programme challenged five contemporary designers to produce a limited edition piece of work drawing inspiration from the original Coca-Cola glass bottle. Recent outdoor advertising also

celebrated the form and style of the Original Glass bottle using the shape of the naked form to bring to life the unique contours of the bottle.

But let us not forget the thirst-quenching drink itself. Coca-Cola has been very cautious about introducing variants of its classic brand. The first was Diet Coke in 1982, which has taken on a life of its own. Flavour variants born out of local consumer insights have also been added – Cherry Coke, Diet Coke with Lemon and Vanilla Coke – but the key is that they are all distinctively 'the real thing'.

coca-cola.co.uk

★converse®

The most iconic street
sneaker in the world

Converse®, the original basketball brand and largest manufacturer of athletic footwear in the US, has been designing high quality athletic footwear and clothing for 95 years.

Today, Converse provides technologically advanced shoes to basketball professionals and supporters worldwide, as well as being worn for its retro style credentials.

The story began back in 1908, when Marquis Converse founded the Rubber Shoe Company. Seven years later the world's first Basketball boot, the Converse All Star®, rolled off the production line. Basketball player Chuck Taylor was signed to the brand as the first ever shoe endorser in history. Having become famous at high school, Chuck progressed to play professionally for the original Celtics, Buffalo Germans and Akron Firestones. In 1921, Chuck Taylor joined the Converse sales team in Chicago while continuing to play, and two years later The Chuck Taylor All Star® was born. Converse has since added a long line of endorsers to its basketball portfolio, including Julius Erving, alias Dr J, and NBA superstar Dennis Rodman.

Service has always been key to the brand's success, and as a result Converse created a loyal clientele of coaches, school and college teams, players and spectators throughout the US. By the late1960s, Converse had a 90% share of the basketball market.

Fast forward to 1996 and president Mickey Bell announced that the All Star Patch would be the focus of Converse's brand positioning, and would appear on the Tribute collection. The All Star 2000 and the Dr J 2000 pay homage to Chuck Taylor as well as Dr J and are the first two styles in the range, with a third currently in production – The All Star 91, which is based on Dennis Rodman's player number.

Back by popular demand, autumn/winter 2003 witnesses the return of the classic prints Hot Rod Flames and Stars and Bars, plus the introduction of a new CND peace logo.

Sure to be a hit with the fashion-conscious Converse fan, also launching in autumn 2003 are the new style calf-length boots, which are available in fabrics and prints including military camouflage and leopard skin. The classic canvas All Stars will also have a new look with bright, two-tone colour schemes.

Former vice president of menswear for Ralph Lauren, John Varvatos, now collaborates with Converse, producing a men's range that combines the brands' signature street-style with the designers' easy elegance.

Converse clothing really sums up the recent trend towards retro styling. For the spring/summer 2003 season, the all-American casual range was inspired by preppy Americana, jocks, greasers and cult film classics: Pink Lady jackets are worn with cute but sexy tight tees, while for boys, the collection draws inspiration from the military, including chunky logo knits and American Air Force leather jackets.

Converse advertises using TV and print –

the most recent campaign being 'The Heritage Factory' featuring the All Star 2000 and Dennis Rodman. However alongside this activity the brand has always been committed to promoting basketball. For example, in 2000 Converse sponsored the biggest street basketball event since the NBA 3-on-3 in 1996, The Converse NBA Jam 2000. It toured around 50 European cities and involved 100,000 basketball fans and featured special guest Dennis Rodman – an old friend of Converse.

House of COURVOISIER.
COGNAC

Alluring amber nectar,
emanating flamboyant opulence

Lying in the south west of France just above Bordeaux, the Cognac region has always had an air of mystery. The very name Cognac is protected by law – and the exact nature of the silky golden spirit that has made the region famous is shrouded in secrecy. For its many aficionados, the richness and sensuality of this splendidly decadent drink is summed up by the brand name COURVOISIER®.

Felix Courvoisier was a respected wine and spirit merchant who – like his father Emmanuel – distributed his product through the Gallois family, key wholesalers based in Bercy (a port just outside Paris). As loyal suppliers to the Imperial Court, the Gallois family had been honoured with a visit by Napoleon to their warehouses in 1811. Legend has it that Napoleon took several barrels of Cognac aboard the HMS Northumberland – the ship that took him on his final journey to St Helen – a rare pleasure much appreciated by English officers, who first called it 'The Brandy of Napoleon'.

It wasn't until 1835 that Felix Courvoisier and Louis Jules Gallois fully merged the businesses that had been founded by their fathers. They set up headquarters in Jarnac, where Chateau Courvoisier is still in operation today. By the early 1900s the brand's identity had firm foundations built. Innovations such as the 'Josephine' bottle shape and the inclusion of the Napoleon silhouette in the logo were introduced. Both of these features can still be seen today.

The brand is now available in over 140 countries and sells more than thirteen million bottles per year. It has won awards such as the Prestige de la France (1983) – the only Cognac to win the country's highest award for excellence – and the International Wine and Spirit Competition, in which Courvoisier XO was named the best Cognac in the world in 1994, and awarded a prestigious gold medal in 2002.

Cognac has always been a noble spirit, representing luxury and tradition. For many years the word conjured up images of country estates and blazing log fires. But as we enter a new era of decadence, these images are fading. The change began when the US hip hop community adopted Cognac as a status symbol, a trend clearly signalled by songs such as Pass The Courvoisier by Busta Rhymes and P Diddy. Sophisticated urbanites are developing a taste for luxury brands that are able to combine their classic roots with a modern temperament.

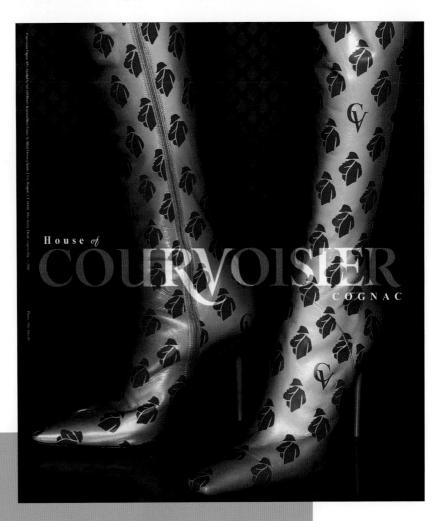

House of
COURVOISIER
COGNAC

Courvoisier's subsequent marketing has reflected this new direction, starting with the House of Courvoisier print campaign in the US in 2000. The innovative campaign successfully linked the brand's heritage with a sociable, fashionable and modern lifestyle. No longer the preserve of dusty wood-panelled rooms, Courvoisier is now a glamorous accessory.

Courvoisier has also forged partnerships in the fashion, music and media worlds. In 2002 Courvoisier was the official spirit of New York Fashion Week, as well as the MOBO Awards after party. It teamed up with The House of Field (from David Dalrymple and Sex and the City stylist Patricia Fields) to create limited edition designer bottles. Furthermore, Courvoisier linked up with Dan MacMillan for the launch of his fashion label Zoltar the Magnificent, and with Agent Provocateur to design lingerie inspired by Napoleon.

Courvoisier's authenticity and legendary quality has ensured that the drink has remained the cognac of choice amongst 'those in the know'.

DAZED
& CONFUSED

Dazed & Confused magazine is the leading independent voice for contemporary creative culture, combining original ideas with visually stunning photography and design. It began life ten years ago as a London based fanzine and has grown to become an internationally known and respected title. Despite its growth it has always remained true to co-founders Jefferson Hack and photographer Rankin's original philosophy of balancing aspirational with inspirational content.

The magazine offers an individualistic reference point for the shape of things in music, film, fashion, arts and design. Dazed explores social issues, politics, architecture and technology. It aims to stand apart from other magazines that conform

to carefully controlled product-led marketing campaigns and does not simply regurgitate standard press releases but digs deep to unearth new talent. In short Dazed sets the agenda. It sets trends. It doesn't follow them.

Dazed is spiritual home to a 50 strong creatively curious crew who are continually pushing at the boundaries of writing, reportage, design and photography. Its eclectic family of contributors has included musicians Björk and Massive Attack, artists Sam Taylor Wood and Jake and Dinos Chapman, fashion designer Alexander McQueen and filmmaker Michael Winterbottom.

The magazine has won plaudits from its readers and the publishing industry alike. Since its 1992 launch Dazed has won a continual flow of awards including Front Cover of the Year and Best Use of Photography in the Magazine Design Awards.

Continuing to grow in revenue and circulation the Dazed publishing group have created a number of brand extensions to ensure they remain at the forefront of creative talent and culture. These encapsulate the title's core values which are to identify and promote emerging creative talent. With this in mind and to coincide with its tenth anniversary Dazed joined forces with Topshop to launch 2002's national student creativity tour and awards. The Re:Creation awards took the magazine on a regional tour of the UK in a specially created double-decker exhibition bus, holding seminars and parties on the way and culminating in a ceremony at the V&A in London. The competition, on the strength of its success, is becoming an annual event, aiming to give young creatives the opportunity they need to succeed in an increasingly tough environment. Elsewhere Dazed has collaborated with online financial services operator Egg for the provision of five artistic bursaries enabling up and coming creatives to realise their personal vision.

As part of the Dazed Group the title remains independent in ownership as well as in spirit. The brand has diversified into other areas successfully exporting the Dazed & Confused style and philosophy. This is true of Dazed Film & TV, which from its launch in 1998 quickly built a reputation for distinctive film and television production.

With the launch of Another Magazine, its luxury fashion bi-annual title, the brand successfully balances the innovation of the style magazine with the sophistication of a luxury magazine. Few other magazines provide such diverse content alongside such poignant and outstanding fashion photography. Made in both New York and London, the magazine brings the international fashion community closer together and continues to interview the seemingly unapproachable and photograph the unbelievable.

Dazed has never shied away from challenging orthodoxies. This is evidenced by support for initiatives such as Stop Esso and Jubilee 2000 through events and editorial as well as featuring controversial fashion pages like its bold Disabled shoot and pictures of models giving blood to raise awareness for the National Blood Association.

Dazed entered the twenty first century without losing touch with its original risk-taking independent ideals. The magazine is now sold in more than 40 markets worldwide and is set to grow further and be the global voice for cutting-edge creative talent.

DENON

Denon is a brand built on original ideas and respected for its superb quality Hi-Fi, Home Cinema and Pro-Audio equipment that brings clarity and definition to both sound and vision.

Denon customers are rewarded with the pride of ownership that comes from nearly a century of superlative audio engineering and outstanding technical innovation. Today the brand is recognised internationally as a leading manufacturer for the professional entertainment and information industries as well as for discerning individuals.

The Denon brand was established in the 1930s and initially developed disc recorders for radio stations. In 1939 Denon introduced the world's first direct-drive studio turntable.

Through the 1950s and 1960s Denon became synonymous with top sound quality among audiophiles and professionals. 1951 for example, witnessed the launch of the world's first stereo moving coil phono cartridge, marking Denon as a pioneer in high-fidelity (Hi-Fi) manufacturing. Denon's technological edge was further sharpened in the 1970s when its engineers developed the world's first commercial digital recorder and released the world's first digital

| A legacy for creating beautiful equipment that provides high quality sound |

music recordings on LP. Then in the 1980s the brand was among the first to introduce CD players and CD software to an excited international market. Furthermore, the world's first commercially available CD's were manufactured by Denon. In 1991 it created the market, which it still dominates, for delivering superb high-quality miniature Hi-Fi systems. The brand passed another milestone in 1997 by releasing the world's first commercial music DVD disc; a live recording of Beethoven's Symphony

No 3 and Chopin's Piano Concerto No 1. With the digital entertainment revolution Denon earned further international acclaim and recognition by applying its high-grade audio technology to home cinema systems. Its latest products bring new levels of quality to home cinema and a sonic realism which literally envelops the listener in sound. In fact Denon has introduced almost every new leading-edge home cinema technology to the market. In the UK Denon has grown from zero in 1983 to become one of the strongest and most respected brands in the quality market, consequently garnering a string of industry and consumer awards along the way. Its twin deck DJ CD players have become the industry standard for clubs, while its professional CD and MiniDisc Players are used in radio stations the world over. In 1994 its Alpha Processor won the European Audio Award for Innovation. In 2002 Denon scooped four categories in What Hi-Fi's prestigious consumer awards including Best Hi-Fi System and at the beginning of 2003 its DVD-A1 was ranked 'best of the best' by Esquire magazine.

   As well as producing the best and some of the most expensive home entertainment systems, Denon sells huge quantities of the highest quality micro and mini systems as well. The brand, therefore, is built on the quality of its products which are recognised and rated by independent specialist retailers and knowledgeable opinion formers. Word of mouth is more important than mega marketing campaigns. Denon dazzles with the excellence of its product, not its advertising spend.

denon.co.uk

DIESEL®
FOR SUCCESSFUL LIVING

Unpredictable, dynamic vitality and energy guided by imagination and passion

Diesel design does not follow established trends. It is largely unaffected by fashion fads; it is innovative and at times a bit radical, but it always shows careful attention to detail and focuses on its selection of quality materials and production techniques. The brand is now present in over 80 countries with more than 200 single-brand stores. It has also attracted some very desirable followers – on a recent cover of Vanity Fair, featuring a clutch of Hollywood's hottest male movie stars, Tom Cruise and Dennis Quaid both sported Diesel jeans.

The Diesel brand was created not by an English eccentric as one might imagine, but by

the Italian duo Renzo Rosso and Andriano Goldschmied in 1978. The name was chosen because the word means exactly the same thing worldwide – an early indication of the company's international aspirations. The brand was launched with a menswear collection in 1979, and by the early 1980s Diesel was already creating a buzz outside its Italian home market. In 1985 Rosso took complete control of Diesel by buying out the other partners and becoming the sole force behind the brand. Thereafter the company began a period of remarkable growth and expansion.

A womenswear line was launched in 1989, and two years later the brand launched its global marketing strategy, with the slogan 'For Successful Living'. Other brand extensions followed with spin-offs such as 55DSL – a skate-punk riff on the Diesel style as well as Diesel Kids. Other off shoots include the art deco Pelican hotel on Miami's renowned South Beach – a three dimensional expression of its funky aesthetic. Each guest room has its own distinctive décor and with titles including 'Best Little Whorehouse', 'Me Tarzan You Vain' or 'A Fortune In Aluminium' you know that this is no travel tavern.

Rosso, also created Diesel Farm nearly ten years ago. The estate of over 100 hectares is situated on the Marostica hills in Italy. It has vineyards producing Diesel branded Chardonnay, Merlot and Cabernet Sauvignon and olive trees from which extra virgin oil is produced. The farm also has 35 hectares of pasture and a vast forest area.

Rosso has raked in a string of awards over the years, including being called 'one of the 100 most important people in the world' by Select magazine. Italy's most prestigious MBA programme described Diesel as "an entrepreneurial phenomenon".

The brand's truly original advertising campaigns began in 1991 and have always been run worldwide. Its ironic appropriation of 1950s advertising vocabulary – suggesting that its products make for a better life – was initially regarded with scepticism by marketing experts, but has proved an enduring theme. The Cannes Lions, Eurobest and Epica are just some of the advertising festivals that have showered awards on Diesel over the past few years. The brand's creative approach doesn't stop with advertising – even its clothing catalogues are celebrated for their radical look, with the products often serving only as incidental content in a highly stylised publication.

Diesel also encourages the creative talents of the future. At present, it is involved in four international projects: Diesel-u-music, a competition for underground musicians; ITS – International Talent Support, a fashion competition for students and young designers; the Pocko project, a pocket-sized art books collection; and the OFFF digital arts festival in Barcelona.

Rosso, who remains the driving force behind Diesel, is still passionate about the brand he has nurtured. He simply says, "Diesel is not my company, it is my life."

diesel.com

DKNY

Since its launch in 1989, the fashion label DKNY has come to represent the energy and spirit of New York. Like the Big Apple, DKNY is international, eclectic and fun. Embracing real life and all its personalities, DKNY was created as the street-wise counterpart to Donna Karan New York, a luxe Collection known for its cashmere and hand-painted devore dresses. She called her new brand DKNY, inspired by the sound and rhythm of FDNY and NYPD, shorthand for New York City's fire and police departments.

From the start, DKNY has always been about fast fashion with an urban mindset. Having previously broken new ground with Donna Karan New York, the designer wanted to dress her other, more casual lifestyle, while keeping a sophisticated edge. "I wanted jeans that would fit and flatter a woman's body," she explains. "Everything out there was designed for boy-like figures and from a very young point of view. I envisioned a collection designed like a real wardrobe, with flexible, interchangeable pieces polished enough to wear one way to work and hip enough to wear another way on the weekend." At the time, such a collection didn't exist. DKNY trail-blazed a new category, called 'bridge' in the fashion industry that lived between designer and inexpensive sportswear.

DKNY has something for every age, mood and lifestyle, from tailored suits and vintage-inspired dresses, to leather

motorcycle jackets and jeans, to yoga-wear and spirited evening wear perfect for clubbing. "DKNY is one-stop shopping," says Karan. "Its all here under one roof, from the classic and timeless to the super trendy and of the moment." DKNY grew so popular and diverse that it gave birth to a family of companies, such as DKNY men, DKNY Jeans, DKNY City, DKNY Active, DKNY Kids, DKNY Underwear, as well as DKNY Eyewear and DKNY Shoes. There are also a myriad of DKNY accessories lines to complement every season, including handbags. Everything has an unmistakable New York sensibility.

Over the years, DKNY has come to represent not only an attitude, but also a lifestyle. DKNY fragrances for men and women were introduced and quickly became bestsellers. A multifaceted home furnishings collection called DKNY Life, created to dress the urban home in fashion textures and innovative accessories, was also launched. DKNY is so tied to NYC, that it's advertising often features Manhattan as a backdrop. DKNY has however exploded out of New York, becoming one of the city's most famous exports. There are now over 50 company owned or licensed DKNY stores worldwide. Since DKNY is as much uptown as it is downtown, there are now two flagship stores in New York City – one on Madison Avenue and 60th Street, the other on West Broadway in SoHo. Both are the spiritual homes of the brand, bringing DKNY back to where it all began.

dkny.com

Dom Pérignon

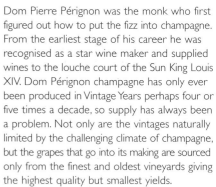

Dom Pierre Pérignon was the monk who first figured out how to put the fizz into champagne. From the earliest stage of his career he was recognised as a star wine maker and supplied wines to the louche court of the Sun King Louis XIV. Dom Pérignon champagne has only ever been produced in Vintage Years perhaps four or five times a decade, so supply has always been a problem. Not only are the vintages naturally limited by the challenging climate of champagne, but the grapes that go into its making are sourced only from the finest and oldest vineyards giving the highest quality but smallest yields.

The quality and the scarcity of Dom Pérignon or D.P. has been the driving force in creating the brand's image. Only distributed via exclusive restaurants and fine wine shops, the wine always scores highly on wine values but equally important on the glamour factor. James Bond's patronage of Dom Pérignon has played a significant role in spreading the fame of the brand. The easy-going

glamour and iconic elegance of 007 and Dom Pérignon seem to be ideally suited to each other.

Since the mid 1990s, Dom Pérignon has focused on sponsoring photography around the world. Recent sponsorships include the Dom Pérignon collections at Hamiltons which have celebrated the works of Doisneau (famed for the Kiss), Horst and most recently David Bailey. This featured classic photographs from the 1960s which included iconic shots of Michael Caine, Mick Jagger, Jean Shrimpton and the Krays.

Co-sponsorship of 2002's acclaimed Mario Testino exhibition at the National Portrait Gallery proved to be one of the best first night parties of the year. The glamorous atmosphere was magnified by the guest list which included the likes of Madonna, Kate Moss, and Stella McCartney.

To celebrate the most recent vintage of Dom Pérignon Rosé, British jewellery designer Stephen Webster was commissioned to create a collection inspired by the champagne. Within the predominantly pink collection he fashioned pink morganites into effervescent bubble cuts and set pink tourmaline into rings to look like corks bursting out of their diamond settings. The centrepiece of the collection is a £5 million diamond, dubbed the 'Magnum Rose', which was set in the shape of the Dom Pérignon star. The concept was to celebrate the shooting star which was said to have shot across the sky before the first vintage of Dom Pérignon was harvested.

Rankin photographed the Dom Pérignon Rosé jewellery collection being worn by six dancers from the Royal Opera House. These images reflect the balance, structure and sensuality which are the key properties of Dom Pérignon.

Although Dom Pérignon is only made in very special years, the role of the winemaker is to ensure that the style of the wine remains consistent. To help with this task, a wine library (oenothèque) is maintained to ensure that the older vintages can be retried over the years as an ongoing reference point. Tiny quantities of these wines are available in Michelin starred restaurants and a handful of London Department stores. The vintages available, which are released from the Dom Pérignon cellars in optimum conditions, are 1988, 1980, 1973, 1964 and the 007 favourite 1959.

DUCATI

Respected for its racing heritage,
technical excellence and sharp design

With a brand image that is undoubtedly the envy of many the world over, Ducati is synonymous with Italian style, design, state of the art engineering and of course racing.

Founded in 1926, the Ducati Company began with the production of radio components with other investors in Bologna. By the 1940s Ducati commanded a global business from the then sprawling factory complex, which was later destroyed during World War II.

Rising from the ashes, Ducati took a different path and began production of small auxiliary motors for bicycles, then motorcycles. With the arrival of pioneering engineer Fabio Taglioni, Ducati's motorcycle production began to get very serious. One of the major highlights of this was the introduction of the innovative 'Desmo' valve gear that is still a unique feature of Ducati motorcycles today.

By the 1980s and early 1990s Ducati reached even greater heights with the introduction of the now legendary Monster range (celebrating its tenth birthday in 2003 with over 130,000 units produced in total) and the luscious Supermono race bike.

1994 saw one of Ducati's most significant motorcycles created – the award winning 916. Collecting numerous design awards around the world, the 916 then began to prove its ability on the race circuits of the world as it moved through its evolution as the 916, 996 and finally the 998. Collecting no less than nine World Superbike riders titles and eleven Constructors titles, Ducati is the most successful manufacturer ever in this production based series.

In the late 1990s Ducati began to expand into accessories and clothing, and with the creation of the Ducati Store concept customers could truly become part of the Ducati family.

Through advertising and public relations the company has created a sense of community amongst fans and owners of the bikes, who are now affectionately labelled 'Ducatisti'. Underlined in 1998 with the first World Ducati Weekend, held in Italy, the event has grown and the third event took place in 2002.

The Ducati website is another key tool, that enables 'Ducatisti' to stay in touch as well as attract new followers. A UK website is now active allowing UK customers to stay updated with news and events closer to home. Forward thinking, Ducati launched the MH900e on the website in 2000, becoming the first motorcycle to be exclusively reserved on the internet.

1999 saw Ducati listed on the New York and Milan stock exchanges, demonstrating just how far the company has come.

Movie Directors continue to request machines for their films, hoping the brand's strong image will rub off on their stars. Recently featured in the Matrix Reloaded, Blade II and Rollerball, Ducati is still the bike for Hollywood.

2002 saw the launch of the 999 Superbike. Instantly recognised as setting a new standard, Ducati managed to once again produce a truly pioneering machine with levels of technology previously unseen.

In 2003 Ducati launched another new concept with the introduction of the truly versatile Multistrada, instantly creating a whole new motorcycle niche.

With the continuation of the 'Ducati People' advertising campaign, Ducati encourage its customers to become involved, giving the advertising an individual and real feel, by showing some seriously cool customers on some of Ducati's most awesome machines.

2003 also saw Ducati launch its comeback in the Grand Prix class after 30 years. What can be described as one of the most competitive forms of motorcycle racing, Ducati have developed a completely new machine - The Desmosedici. By the sixth race of the championship Ducati had secured two podium finishes and one win with Loris Capirossi, making Ducati the first non Japanese manufacturer to win in the now Moto GP championship.

ducatiuk.com

GAGGIA®

As any coffee connoisseur will tell you, espresso is all about the 'crema'. This is the delicate, unbroken, golden brown foam that covers the surface of every perfect espresso, obscuring the powerful black core of the coffee beneath. And we owe the creation of the 'crema' to Gaggia.

Achille Gaggia unveiled his first coffee machine on September 5th 1938. It was his ingenious idea of forcing water under pressure to flow over the coffee grounds – instead of the usual method of blasting them with steam – that produced this 'crema'.

Gaggia went on to officially found his coffee machine company in 1947, and since then the brand has become synonymous throughout the world with authentic Italian coffee. Over the years the machines have evolved from the traditional manually operated devices, with a lever controlling a water-pressurising piston, to fully automated marvels that can grind, measure and deliver a delicious cup of espresso at the flick of a switch.

A crucial chapter in the development of the brand came with the introduction of the Baby Gaggia in 1977. The first domestic coffee machine, its launch capitalised on the rise in popularity of espresso during the 1970s. For the first time,

The crème de la crème of coffee machines

it was possible to create in your own home an espresso to rival those being sipped in cafés. The Baby Gaggia established the brand at the forefront of the domestic machine market, a position it retains to this day.

All Gaggia machines are made in the Robecco sul Naviglio factory in Milan, and are designed to combine tradition with technology. Two of the latest models include the G Series and the Concetto. The G Series is the first commercial Gaggia machine to feature an electrically heated cup-warming area and a thermally activated safety switch. But espresso addicts will be more appreciative of its retro Italian design, featuring a glossy plastic casing moulded into G-shaped curves. Available in gold, deep red or electric blue, the G Series provides restaurateurs with the perfect combination of functionality and style.

Meanwhile, the Concetto is designed for more modest outlets. Its modular design provides interchangeable units for cappuccino, espresso, hot water and steam, meaning that it can be easily adapted to any restaurant environment. Once again, design is key, and the Concetto comes in a traditional faded bronze hue.

Proudly displayed in restaurants and bars across the globe, gleaming Gaggia machines prove their worth and act as their own marketing tools. But the brand also has a trade communications programme to raise awareness of new and existing products. As well as issuing press materials and photographs, the company regularly loans out machines to trade shows and magazine reviewers and enjoys media coverage which spans consumer and trade publications, radio and television broadcasts, and online media.

However Gaggia's reputation has primarily built its name through quality, design and a passion for making the perfect espresso – every time.

gaggia.uk.com

Goldsmiths
UNIVERSITY
OF LONDON

A hothouse for creative talent

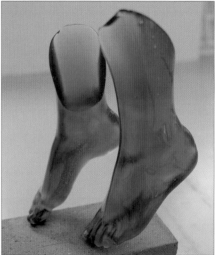

Situated in South-East London, Goldsmiths College, University of London has, over the years, nurtured some of the finest creative talents in the realms of fine art, design, drama, the media, music, politics and entertainment. In doing so it has established an international reputation not only for its high academic standards but also the characters that have blossomed as a result of their Goldsmiths experience. The College is proud of its defining liberal and creative approach which is taken in the teaching of all subjects – not just the arts.

Founded in 1891 and part of the University of London since 1904, Goldsmiths has defined artistic movements for many generations and can claim to be the UK's leading creative university. With a reputation that precedes it – particularly in the arts, social sciences and humanities – the College offers a broad range of undergraduate, postgraduate, professional and adult education programmes and undertakes world-class research and practice. Key to Goldsmiths' success to-date is the emphasis it places on teaching led by pioneering research and an innovative outlook that carries through to all areas of study and across all departments.

With approximately 6,000 full-time students and 4,000 students on short courses, many of them from overseas, this cosmopolitan university has seen a number of influential alumni pass through its doors including Lucian Freud, Damien Hirst, John Cale, Bridget Riley, Gillian Wearing, Mary Quant, Molly Parkin, Blur's Alex James, Julian Clary and Malcolm McLaren.

Contemporary galleries such as Tate Modern are bursting with the work of Goldsmiths alumni. Since it began over ten years ago, four winners of the Turner Prize, and almost a quarter of those shortlisted for the award, have been Goldsmiths graduates. In addition, past students have also been credited with starting the Young British Artists 'YBA' movement.

Goldsmiths is part of the prestigious '94 Group' of smaller research-oriented universities who are committed to international standards of excellence and striving to be at the forefront of creative, cognitive, cultural and social processes.

Industry awards and accolades are a regular occurrence for the university which is regarded by many as the most innovative for the arts in Europe. In a recent, independently judged, quality assessment of its research, two departments gained the coveted top grading of 5*, namely Media and Communications (one of only two such departments in the country to receive this rating) and Sociology.

Goldsmiths' creative ethos is also reflected in its student recruitment materials, including the prospectuses and the video. The College has won over twelve awards in recent years, nationally and internationally, from the prestigious Communicators in Business Award, the Case Circle of Excellence Awards to HEIST UK Awards for Education Marketing, making it the most prolific award winner of any UK university.

Committed to providing the best, most advanced facilities for study and research, work has begun on phase one of a new Arts Complex designed by Alsop Architects. Phase one is due to open by the end of 2004, and will provide state-of-the-art facilities to develop the interaction between the arts and social sciences for the influencers of the future.

goldsmiths.ac.uk

H&M

Fast moving affordable fashion

H&M has built its reputation by offering a combination of high fashion and low prices. It is now one of Europe's largest fashion retailer's and has more than 849 stores in seventeen countries from Austria to the US, with the centre of operations still in its birthplace – Sweden. It is therefore a great achievement to be rated as a 'cool' brand.

H&M was conceptualised by Erling Persson in 1947. His inspiration came from a trip he took to the US where he saw clothing stores which offered good quality items at low prices. It struck him that this American dream would go down well in his native Sweden.

Persson chose the brand name, 'Hennes', the Swedish word for 'hers' which reflected his offering of women's clothing. In these early days ranges included party dresses in rayon with shirt bodices and big fluffy skirts.

The company expanded steadily and in 1968 Persson bought Mauritz Widforss, a hunting and gun store with premises in Stockholm. Bizarrely the property came with a supply of men's clothing. Persson saw this as new potential and from here progressed the menswear range. He also changed the brand name to Hennes & Mauritz to incorporate a sense of this new direction.

The brand's success continued during the 1980s and 1990s and rapid expansion saw Hennes & Mauritz arrive on the international scene. For the first time an in-house design team was established and jewellery and accessories were created to complement the clothing lines. It was also at this juncture that the brand name was shortened to H&M as we now know it.

Collections for children and teenagers have joined the ranges for women and men. Concepts that shape the direction of the brand include updated classics and fashion basics to the very trendiest of clothes for slick urbanites. More recently further ranges have been added including a line for pregnant women – 'MAMA', as well as BiB, which stands for 'Big is Beautiful' and offers 'plus-size' fashion up to a size 30. The brand has also successfully launched an own-brand cosmetics line.

H&M's philosophy of fashion, quality and price, is reinforced by its ethical policies. It doesn't make clothes that may be perceived as provocative on small children. It does not stock 'war-inspired' garments – so camouflage prints are out, and it won't carry messages or patterns on clothing that are deemed to be offensive, racist, sexist, political or religious. In 1997 H&M developed a 'Code of Conduct' which all H&M suppliers must comply to. The code includes requirements concerning the working environment, a ban on child labour, fire safety, working hours, wages and freedom of association.

H&M sees its stores as key to communicating with its customers. It therefore aims to create attractive and inspiring environments where customers can feel at home, while being excited in their exploration of the store.

One of the company's greatest strengths is that it ensures that there is something new in each store, every day. The brand also maintains a balance between the updated classic clothing and ultra high fashion looks that are brought in almost as soon as new styles are a hit with the fashionista. H&M buys garments during each season, not just at the start, which means better 'fashion accuracy'. Certain trends are predicted up to a year in advance in regards to colours, fabrics and design. The very latest trends are picked up at much shorter notice.

H&M communicates in many different ways through the media, on billboards, in press ads, in TV and cinema commercials as well as on the internet. It sees the purpose of its advertising as being an inspiring invitation to its stores. H&M continues to be an invite that fashion lovers can't refuse.

hm.com

haⲭkasan

Walking down the neon-lit passage that is London's Hanway Street on a summer evening, you could be forgiven for thinking that you have been transported into an exotic film noir. The feeling becomes more powerful as you approach the heavily draped entrance of Hakkasan. Then London dematerialises altogether and you are in Hong Kong, or perhaps Shanghai. Inside, the atmosphere is somewhere between a hi-tech opium den, a twenty first century speakeasy, and a Chinese restaurant adrift in space.

It is no surprise to learn that Hakkasan's creator, the restaurateur Alan Yau, was born in the New Territories of Hong Kong. In a very real sense, Yau returned to his roots with Hakkasan.

The name offers a powerful clue – 'Hakka' is Yau's native dialect and 'San' is a respectful Japanese form of address. Even the Hakkasan logo – which crops up on matchbooks, menus and stationery – employs a back-to-back K that echoes the Chinese symbol for good fortune.

With its vast sixteen metre bar and aquatic lighting effects (the logo also recalls the symbol for water), Hakkasan exudes an atmosphere of relaxed decadence. Lattice screens give the huge space a discreetly labyrinthine quality. In fact, Hakkasan plays several roles: as well as the lounge bar, Ling Ling, there's a 130-cover restaurant serving Dim Sum during the day, with an A La Carte menu of modern Chinese cuisine at night.

After extensive research, Yau appointed Tong Chee Hwee as head chef. Tong arrived direct from the Summer Pavilion, the famed Chinese

restaurant at the Ritz Carlton in Singapore. He brought with him his sous chef and master Dim Sum chef, Cheong Wah Soon. Dim Sum can also be nibbled in Ling Ling to accompany one of the numerous cocktails – many with an Asian theme – or a glass of wine from the extensive list.

As always in an Alan Yau restaurant, design is vital to Hakkasan's appeal. Yau again collaborated with Christian Liaigre, probably the most influential interior designer in France. Famed for his renovation of the Hotel Montalembert in Paris and Manhattan's Hotel Mercer, Liaigre had previously produced the dark wooden interior of Yau's Busaba Eathai restaurant in Wardour Street.

Yau wanted to move away from stark minimalism that characterised progressive Oriental restaurants in the 1990s and 'bring back the dragon' by creating an exciting and atmospheric interior. Liaigre's response was to translate traditional Chinese motifs, such as lanterns and screens, into a more contemporary design vocabulary. The huge bar is made of dark-stained English oak, as are the tables, screens and latticing. These strike a contrast with the lighter tones of lilac and baby blue in the leather seating, the low white marble tables and the blue glass which is used in mirrors, back lit panels and shelving. Pendulum Chinese lanterns punctuate the overhead space and an extraordinary wall of sawn slate provides a dramatic backdrop to the nocturnal bar activity. Lighting technician Arnold Chan at Isometrix provided the otherworldly illumination.

To complement the interior design, two of London's leading fashion designers created uniforms worn by staff. The waiting staff swishes about in Hussein Chalayan, while the management sports Oswald Boateng.

In common with many cutting-edge brands, Hakkasan relies chiefly on word-of-mouth to build its reputation. It does not have a website or actively carry out any form of marketing yet its reputation and press coverage is outstanding.

In 2003, not only was Hakkasan acclaimed as the Best Oriental Restaurant in London at the Carlton TV London Restaurant Awards, but it also became the only Chinese restaurant in the UK and one of only three in Europe to boast a Michelin Star.

A sophisticated and exclusive club with an informal air

Situated in an historic Georgian townhouse in a central London square, Home House has been providing sumptuous private club facilities to a discerning clientele since February 1999.

At Home House, the sheer splendour of the Georgian architecture, combined with the discreet, but unstuffy ambience makes it the number one choice for celebrity bashes and sees A-list stars such as Madonna taking time out to relax on a regular basis.

This glamorous building was built in 1776 by James Wyatt and Robert Adam for the rich socialite Elizabeth, Countess of Home, as a party venue, and was also home to the French Embassy in 1782. After lying derelict for ten years, it was lovingly restored in the late 1990s as the private member's club it now is.

Home House has become established as one of the world's leading private member's clubs. The brains behind the brand is its managing director and former Savoy director Brian Clivaz, whose attention-to-detail and passion for excellent customer service has successfully turned Home House into a modern incarnation of its former self; it is a haven of socialising and schmoozing for the fashionable and successful.

Home House has a definite air of English eccentricity about it, and in keeping with this is the clubs' similarly quirky logo features a crocodile

caricature complete with crown and walking cane. This appears in all the club's communications, often embossed in silver, as well as in fabric form in each bedroom.

The food at Home House is masterminded by head chef Adrian Martin using fresh ingredients that echo the English seasons. It is truly exquisite and has been applauded by members, visitors and critics alike. Meanwhile, the carefully thought-out wine list includes French, European and New World wines from some of the world's greatest names.

The Bison Bar which lies at the heart of the club has deep, welcoming chairs and sofas, classic cocktails, cigars and renowned club sandwiches – all of which can be enjoyed by members. The Drawing Room and the Front Parlour evoke classic, eighteenth century glamour. There is even a private eighteenth century walled garden for discreet, al fresco entertaining and dining which carries a lively buzz in the air – English weather permitting.

And after an evening of wallowing in such splendour, one can retire to one of the eighteen lavishly decorated bedrooms which reflect the many famous people who have lived or stayed at the address in the past. Each is individually decorated in Art Deco, Georgian, Gothic and Oriental styles and comes complete with Egyptian cotton sheets, goose down pillows and hand-made mattresses made by Savior Beds and the business essentials required to stay in touch with the outside world. The designer bathrooms have all the latest creature comforts (including a squeezy belly crocodile).

For those who want to work off the excesses of the night before, the Italian tiled Turkish bath and state-of-the-art health spa, which is situated in the former servants quarters below stairs, offers all the latest exercise equipment, massage therapies, beauty treatments as well as pilates classes.

With a word-of-mouth reputation that precedes itself and a waiting list of over 1,400 would-be members, Home House continues to go from strength to strength. The latest venture for managing director Brian Clivaz is the acquisition of the famous Mayfair fish restaurant, Scott's, 20 Mount Street, which he has re-established back to its former glory. The Penguin Bar is the new addition to Scott's Restaurant, which is an exclusive private bar for Home House members and Scott's clientele.

homehouse.co.uk

JAGUAR

Ever since its first wholly designed and built motor car, the legendary SS, hit the road in 1935, Jaguar has established a reputation for creating some of the world's most beautiful high-performance sports cars. It's a dynasty which includes timeless classics – cars which not only set new benchmarks in design and technology but became part of the British identity.

Who can forget the E-TYPE? The essence of 1960s cool and a true ground-breaking design in its day. And then there was the Mk II saloon – the archetypal 'cops and robbers' car, and star of the hit TV series 'Inspector Morse'. The list can go on – the XK120, the XJ saloon and the XJ220, in its day the fastest production car in the world – are all icons not only of the automotive industry, but of Britain itself.

With legends such as this, Jaguar was helping to establish notions of 'Cool Britannia' long before the phrase hit the headlines in the mid 1990s. Jaguar's performance, panache and superb craftsmanship has long made it a favourite with the style-conscious – Clark Gable and

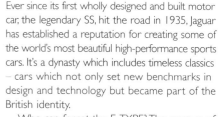

Born to perform

Frank Sinatra were both enthusiasts of the marque, together with many of their Hollywood contemporaries.

'Grace, space and pace' were among the values laid down for Jaguar by its founder, Sir William Lyons, and the series of long, low and elegant models that have distinguished the marque ever since have lived up to that promise. 'Born to perform' is the latest way in which Jaguar chooses to express its brand, but the cars have always spoken for themselves.

Perhaps no more so than the latest generation XK sports cars. First introduced in 1996, the XK8 set new standards in the luxury car market. Available in coupé or convertible form, it has since gone on to become Jaguar's best-selling sports car ever.

And the car has recently been made even better with the 2003 launch of new versions of the 4.2 litre V8 XK8 and the supercharged XKR. Retaining the same classic styling, the new generation XK is a very different animal under the skin, with a more powerful engine, an extensively revised powertrain and a host of other engineering advances. With an XKR 0-60mph performance of just 5.2 seconds (6.0 seconds for the XK8) the new XK is a truly thrilling sports car in the best Jaguar tradition.

The XK8 performed a starring role in the film 'Die Another Day', sharing the platform with another icon of British style and excitement, James Bond. It was also used in the Bond-spoof, Austin Powers, 'The Spy Who Shagged Me'.

During the last ten years, under the ownership of Ford Motor Company (which acquired Jaguar in 1989) the marque has gone from strength to strength, with an increasing product range. The XJ saloon continues to be the

flagship (and was recently re-launched featuring a cutting-edge aluminium-intensive design), but the family is now broader. The mid-range S-TYPE sports saloon (the design of which pays tribute to the 1960s Mk II classic) and the X-TYPE compact saloon have taken the brand into new territory and are helping ensure 'the cat' remains very much on the prowl and more accessible than ever.

jaguar.com

KANGOL

One of the most recognised hat brands around, Kangol graces the heads of the 'in-crowd', pop stars and actors alike. It is famed for its berets, Bermuda Casuals and 504 caps, which Samuel L Jackson sported in the Tarantino film, Jackie Brown.

The brand was founded by Russian Jacques Henryk Spreiregen, who began making berets in the Lake District in 1938. The Kangol brand name was allegedly put together using the K from silK, Knitting or Knitted, the ANG from angora and the OL from wool. The brand grew successfully, with the mid 1950s seeing the birth of the homeboy's favourite 504 cap. Following this, the 1960s had everyone from the Beatles to Pierre Cardin and Mary Quant wearing Kangol creations.

Up until the early 1980s, the kangaroo didn't feature in the brand logo. Its inclusion was prompted not only by imitators that were starting to enter the market, but by a Chinese whisper style mistake. In the US people were asking for 'kangaroo', rather than Kangol hats and caps. To clear up this confusion and detach the brand from the competition, the kangaroo was added to the logo.

Expansion in the 1990s saw the introduction of clothing, footwear, bags and eyewear, which were (and still are) embraced by celebrity fans including Jude Law, De La Soul, Macy Gray and Outkast. This A-list endorsement, in addition to one-off selective advertising in the style press, is considered by Kangol to be more effective in reaching the brand's target audience than traditional advertising.

Currently, the brand is broken down into three categories – Blue, Red and White – inspired by patriotism and the colours of the Union Jack.

Worn by Missy Elliot, Samuel L Jackson, Madonna, Kelly Osbourne and Jay-Z, Blue signifies the classic Kangol and includes the Heritage collection. Named 'Blue' because the hats were originally for blue collar workers, the first 100% wool beret was made in 1938 and is now in the Blue Heritage Range, along with Kangol classics in modern colours, as well as more traditional styles. The old skool hip-hop style hats are also included in Kangol Blue, as are the Enfields that the Beatles wore. New additions for Autumn/Winter 2003 include distressed leather flat caps and trilby's and a new invention called pressed felt as well as luxury wool. Also returning are some of the best Furgora styles from the past, all of which are influenced by the 1960s.

Red signifies the experimental Kangol, and is about new ideas; whether it's producing a hat inspired by a trend, or designing a great hat to wear while searching for surf on England's Westcoast. Kangol Red for Autumn/Winter 2003 features the slacker beanie constructed from the new 'wool with holes', while 504s and pull-ons feature the kangaroo symbol in a graffiti style. Kangol Red is only supplied to the most directional retailers, such as Selfridges and Urban Outfitters.

Kangol White is a platform for other design talents and has previously been designed by Katherine Hamnett, Bella Freud, YMC, Heather Allan and 6876. The collection is currently being designed by Hamish Morrow, who also designed the Spring/Summer 2003 White range. His second range reworks timeless classics – the trilby, trucker cap, cloche and flat cap using satin camo prints and random quilted satin. A heavier wool is used and the trademark kangaroo is glamorised with Swarovski crystals. Kangol White hats are collector's items as they are made on limited runs and never repeated. They can be sought out in stores such as Selfridges and Harvey Nichols. Markus Lupfer is working on the Spring/Summer 2004 and Autumn/Winter 2004 White collections, while the later part of 2004 sees footwear, watches and clothing collections being launched.

With the use of these three distinctive concepts, Kangol continues to innovate with the breadth and depth of its collection and furnish the most stylish heads around.

KURT GEIGER

Elegant, distinctively glamorous
and exuberates quality

The brand name Kurt Geiger has more than a hint of continental sophistication about it; but in fact the shoe and accessory retailer has a distinctly British heritage. This curious blend is the result of the brand's founders, Kurt and Irmgard Geiger, move from their native Austria to England, where they opened their first West End store in 1963. While the brand went through several changes of ownership over the following years, it retained its positioning as a purveyor of luxurious, well-crafted products.

But great brands also have to evolve, and Kurt Geiger was relaunched in 2001 with a new identity created by Wink Media, the consultancy headed by former Wallpaper editor Tyler Brulé. In the same year, three stand-alone stores were opened in London, Leeds and Manchester. The breathtaking interiors and exclusive product ranges reflected a new, modern, confident and sophisticated direction.

The end of May 2003 saw the opening of the tenth Kurt Geiger stand-alone store on Kensington High Street. The store interior takes inspiration from the tone of Kurt Geiger's advertising campaigns and is in tune with its corporate identity: sleek and glamorous contemporary finishes combined with retro influences.

As well as its freestanding stores, Kurt Geiger has 100 concessions, including outlets at Harrods, Liberty and Selfridges. Each outlet is continually monitored to ensure that it is keeping track with its target market. Merchandisers profile every location on an individual basis, to ensure the right product goes to the right store.

The Kurt Geiger range of sleek women's shoes and classic-but-contemporary men's designs have made it one of the world's most respected footwear brands. Like its customers, its products are grown-up and glamorous. Kurt Geiger customers can expect the use of quality materials, whether it's leather (plain or patent), suede, silk, Swarovski crystals, or reptile skins.

The brand's advertising aims to underpin the messages sent out by its products. Its bold campaigns, which initially seemed to challenge perceptions of the brand, have now become the subject of high expectations. The 'Boudoir' campaign of Autumn/Winter 2002, and in particular the brand's pink ballerina stiletto, received an unprecedented level of customer and industry feedback. The South Molton Street store had, at one point, a waiting list of 90 for this one style, which has become something of a signature shoe. The brand also sees window displays as part of its marketing, exporting the atmosphere of its advertising campaigns onto the streets.

Kurt Geiger products are also a favourite amongst national newspaper fashion supplements and titles such as Vogue, Marie Claire and Elle. Indeed, Kurt Geiger built a solid partnership with British Vogue in 2002, becoming the exclusive sponsor of the magazine's first Ultimate Shoe Guide. Kurt Geiger house and external brands occupied 24 of the 100 pages, and gained significant editorial mentions.

Kurt Geiger's obsession with quality is equally evident behind the scenes. Its dedicated Designers/Buyers are constantly travelling the world in search of inspiration. The company invests heavily in staff development, and established an Education and Development Department in 2000 to ensure high levels of customer service and a clear vision of the brand. A direct outcome of this was the Customer Care Charter, which was created by staff and sets the minimum standard of care each customer should receive. However, the company stresses that it does not seek spiel-spinning salespeople, but individuals who can draw on their own personalities to make each customer feel special.

Finally, Kurt Geiger strives to ensure that the reality of the brand is consistent with its image. The company believes that if consumers are lured into a store by advertising or a shop window, their experience of the environment, service, products – and ultimately their purchase – should exceed their expectations.

kurtgeiger.com

Lambretta

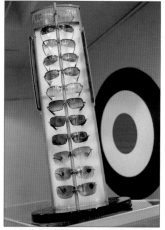

Post-mod retro style

Think Lambretta and the scene casts back to Lambrete, Milan 1947 – the setting for the launch of Ferdinando Innocenti's 123cc engine scooter. The Lambretta, named after the town of its conception, was an instant hit with the Italians. So much so that Ferdinando soon began exporting the scooter across the world. In 1951 the first Lambretta hit British shores and by 1959 the brand was outstripping sales of Vespas – scooters that were already established in the UK. With ideal timing British mod culture arrived and a need for rebellion took hold of the country's youth. Mods and Rockers went to war, fuelled by their opposing taste in music, clothing and lifestyles. And how better for Mods to chase Rockers than on their Lambrettas. Despite its Italian origins, the Lambretta brand had by now adopted a very English personality: the Union Jack and the scooters went hand in hand.

The Lambretta scooter is now no longer in production (although still hugely popular on streets around the globe) however the Lambretta brand and its values continue to thrive. Still embedded at the heart of youth culture, Lambretta clothing has become one of the most sought after fashion labels in the UK and abroad. Since its inception as a clothing label

in 1997, Lambretta has now grown into a global lifestyle brand. In addition to its menswear and womenswear, the range now comprises footwear and accessories including watches, sunglasses and bags.

Famed for the ubiquitous parka, this 'must-have' is now synonymous with the Lambretta name and a sell out every winter. For the Autumn/Winter 03 collection the brand created different versions including a denim fishtail, a khaki fishtail with a fur-trimmed hood and a distinct camouflage style, pre-orders for which had already been taken in spring.

Always seeking to create something distinctive for its customer, Lambretta also launched a premium 'GP' collection in Autumn/Winter 2002. This collection celebrates the 'Lambretta Grand Prix' scooter, which is the most sought after of all Lambretta scooters and is only made available to a limited number of the UK's leading fashion retailers.

Lambretta's flagship store opened on Carnaby Street in 1997; followed by the opening of a further store in the Victoria Quarter, Leeds, then by a third in Covent Garden, London, which opened in February 2002.

The atmospherics of the stores provide a stylish, airy and contemporary showcase for the Lambretta collections and are painted in a signature Lambretta 'Mint'. However, Lambretta has recently redesigned the Carnaby Street store and personally developed its own 'Lambretta Blue'. All the stores contain Lambretta scooters, including a limited edition two-seater which is rotated between the stores.

The continued success of the Lambretta brand is confirmed by ongoing approval from celebrity wearers in the world of music, film and TV, including members of Stereophonics and Groove Armada, Ewan McGregor and Vernon Kay, to name but a few.

Now considered as one of the 'Great British Labels' Lambretta's latest ad campaign, for its Spring/Summer 2003 season entitled 'The Great British Summer', depicts what the brand bills as its 'most stylish and sophisticated collection to date'. Appearing in such style publications as The Face, Dazed & Confused, Sleazenation, Jack, FHM Collections, amongst others, this campaign has been Lambretta's highest profile ever.

lambrettaclothing.co.uk

> Guts and authenticity with a sense of adventure but a handle on style

Land Rover is one of the few brands that has not one but two iconic products in its range, products recognised the world over by their silhouette alone – Defender, the successor to the original Land Rover, and Range Rover. Arguably, with its characteristic stepped roof line, Discovery is well on its way to becoming a third.

Launched in 1947 as a stopgap product by the Rover Car Company, the original Land Rover quickly established a ready market for its 'go anywhere' capabilities. Used by farmers and construction companies, armies and explorers, Land Rovers helped open up and develop vast areas of the third world in the 1950s and 1960s.

Defender's iconic shape is now being taken up by a whole new generation of users – the streetwise urban traveller. Dressed with alloy wheels, chequer plate trim and colours never seen before on this erstwhile utility vehicle, editions such as the SV90, Tomb Raider and Defender Black versions have found a new audience with buyers who are more interested in design and fashion than with functional excellence.

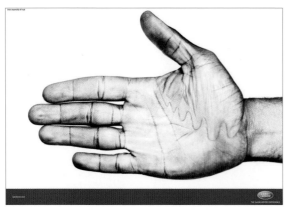

Range Rover was launched in 1970 as an upmarket farming station wagon, at home in the fields but with a greater level of comfort and on road performance compared to its utility brother. Rapturously received for its style and look, however, Range Rover quickly became adopted by the rural set and country gentry as the must-have vehicle for all occasions. So admired was its style that the French even displayed a Range Rover body shell in the Louvre museum in Paris as a piece of art.

A four door version was launched in 1980 and, aided by a limited edition in association with Vogue magazine, the Range Rover was progressively pushed further and further upmarket, gaining new devotees in urban, business and design

sectors. Updated in 1994, after 25 years, the third generation Range Rover was launched to international acclaim in 2002 with an updated, classic style, arresting new front end design and a stunning interior proclaimed by many as the finest of any automobile on the market. Jeremy Clarkson even claimed the new Range Rover had "the power of a volcano, the presence of God, and is probably the best car in the world."

Discovery was Land Rover's entrant into the newly emerging 4x4 leisure market in 1989 and was the best selling 4x4 until 1998. Its combination of power and economy coupled with style and versatility was class leading, and successive updates in 1994 and 1998 kept it as the benchmark in its sector.

Freelander was added to the Land Rover range in 1997 as the company's first compact 4x4 and from 1998 became Europe's top seller. Even today, after seven years in this extremely competitive market, Freelander is still the UK's best selling 4x4.

Unlike many brands, Land Rover is a cluster brand, non linear in nature, offering product designs and experiences to discreet areas in the 4x4 marketplace – utility, luxury, urban and leisure. This cluster nature allows each model to be positioned to appeal to a specific group of customers and also facilitates the introduction of additional products to bring new customers to the brand.

Over the years Land Rover's communications have garnered many awards and memorable television advertising campaigns, such as Defender 'DamBusters' and Freelander 'Born Free', still have huge recall even today.

In March the inaugural Land Rover G4 Challenge was held. Featuring four products, four time zones, four regions and four seasons around the world, sixteen international challengers competed. Endurance, intelligence, team work and driving skills were all required to win the challenge and a G4 Range Rover.

LAVAZZA
ITALY'S FAVOURITE COFFEE

'Espress Yourself' with Italian
sophistication and spirit

As hip and Italian as a Rome coffee bar in a Fellini movie, Lavazza has created and instilled many qualities that make drinking an espresso such a sublimely satisfying experience.

Like many great brands, Lavazza has risen from humble beginnings to become a top international brand. Luigi Lavazza was a farmer's son, but he was so determined to better himself that he took night classes in business studies whilst holding down a series of jobs as a manual labourer, factory worker and shop assistant. He founded The Lavazza Company in 1895 as an all-purpose grocery store in Turin. Very soon, though, he noticed a demand for one special product – coffee. He realised that by roasting and selling this increasingly popular beverage, he could differentiate his store from others. By the end of the nineteenth century, the business developed an enviable reputation as a provider of first-class coffee.

Over the following decades, The Lavazza Company survived two world wars and severe fluctuations in coffee prices by constantly refining both its product and its business strategy. Luigi had realised early on that the secret to establishing a strong brand was to roast and blend coffee from different origins, thus creating a distinctive flavour. At the same time, he expanded and modernised distribution – at the dawn of the automobile age, Lavazza was the first Italian company to deliver fresh coffee on trucks. Later, it introduced the first vacuum packed tins.

Lavazza really came into its own in the 1950s, a boom period for cafés and coffee consumption. It also marked the company's first serious advertising, which used the line 'Lavazza: Paradiso in tazza' (Paradise in a cup). When Luigi's marketing-savvy grandson Emilio joined the company in 1957, Lavazza began its long-standing relationship with the advertising agency Armando Testa, which remains to this day. In the 1960s, Lavazza and Amando Testa spotted the potential of Carosello, a half-hour slot on Italian TV consisting entirely of commercials. Avoiding the hard sell, and always offering entertainment to the public, the pair created animated characters called Caballero and Carmencita. These loveable, conical figures reflected the South American origins of coffee.

Lavazza then employed the Italian actor Nino Manfredi as a brand spokesman, later turning to celebrities such as Luciano Pavarotti and Monica Vitti.

It was however the introduction of the Lavazza calendars that strengthened the brand's cool credentials and the bond between its communication and visual arts. Helmut Newton shot the first in 1993, infusing it with the style, sensuality and vigour that set the template for subsequent shoots. The likes of Ellen Von Unwerth, Elliott Erwitt, Martine Franck, and no less than twelve different photographers from Magnum, the legendary picture agency founded by Robert Capa and Henri Cartier-Bresson have worked with Lavazza.

Since 2002 the calendar shoot also formed the basis for a press and poster advertising campaign for the first time. Using the line 'Espress Yourself', which reflects Lavazza's international positioning of leading espresso brand, together with its spirit of promoting free artistic expression, the bright, fresh and quirky images were conjured up by David LaChapelle. The 2003 campaign, based on the same premise, was shot by Jean-Baptiste Mondino and featured on billboards across Europe. Powerful and elegant, with an international appeal, the ads reflect the current and future evolution of Lavazza, Italy's favourite coffee, into a global brand.

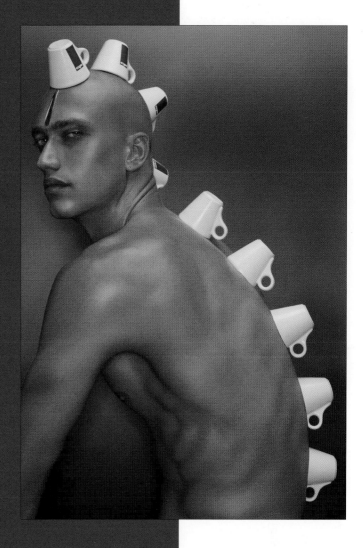

lavazza.com

Ⓜ ANUMISSION

A revolutionary carnival
for debauched hedonists

Manumission is like no other
party on earth. It is a truly
multi-media experience and
a visionary convergence of
different forms of entertainment
that is genuinely unique and has
transformed the concept of
'clubbing' in the way that Cirque
du Soleil revolutionised circus.

2003 saw Manumission's
tenth summer in Ibiza take place every Monday night in Privilege, which
according to the Guinness Book of Records is 'The World's Biggest
Club'. For the 2003 season, it boasted a full working theatre with
a cast and crew of 150, comprising a troupe of fifteen Cuban acrobats,
an aerial performance team from the UK's best Circus Performance
School, Genco, and the 50 famously saucy Manumission Girls. The
stage set was designed by Mark Fisher, who has previously designed
sets for the Rolling Stones, U2, Pink
Floyd and the American Superbowl.

Each year, Manumission has a
theme, and for 2003 it was the
Phantasmagorical Manumission
Mystery. Everyone in the club was
considered to be a suspect and party
hosts Mike and Claire Manumission
turned amateur sleuths, and via the
medium of film, theatre, acrobatics,
song and dance, they unravelled
a series of kinky eco-crimes and
unmasked the true villain.

Musically, Manumission paints on
an amazingly broad canvas. The three rooms enable it to embrace
everything from electro-pop to cabaret, and from tough house
to glam thrash, and 2003 saw the return of live music to Privilege.
Manumission even commissioned some remixes of cult classics,
in line with the theme, and Mike and Claire also sung a version
of the very apt, 'Anything Goes'.

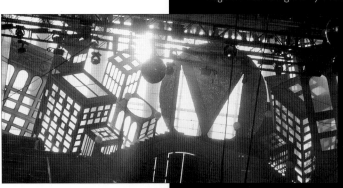

The secret of Manumission's success has been a series of imaginative and inspired innovations. It was Manumission that first introduced the concept of the after-hours 'Carry On', which takes place every Tuesday morning at Space; and the concept of door fees in Ibiza to enable more flamboyant production and an increased number of performers; Manumission is also notorious for introducing the sex show to Ibiza; and was also the only party to refuse to bow to the cult of the overpriced superstar DJ, opting instead to favour a strong set of resident DJs, believing that the public cared more about the party vibe than who was on the decks. The recent demise of the superclubs has borne out this belief.

In 2003, Manumission again stayed ahead of the crowd by stopping production of flyers for the first time in its ten years on the island. Instead, Manumission produced a free, A5 28-page, black and white programme/magazine that sets the scene for the night's events.

Manumission has come a long way since Mike and Andy McKay launched it at a 400-capacity club in Manchester in the early 1990s but it is still a small, family-owned business that the brothers run with their partners, Claire and Dawn. They also own the most successful pre-club bar in Ibiza, Bar M, but Manumission has retained its aura of mystique by refusing to do events outside of Ibiza or advertise.

Nowadays, it is a heaving carnival for the senses. A party that attracts 8,000 revellers every week, including outrageous fashionistas, debauched hedonists and switched-on celebrities. Manumission literally means 'freedom from slavery'. To date, over one million people have opened their minds to Manumission's individual form of liberty.

MATTHEW WILLIAMSON

Vibrant bohemian elegance
loved by the A-list

Since his debut show, Williamson's collections
have continued to strengthen and cement his
reputation as one of London's premiere design
talents. He has also established a very strong client
list which includes Sarah Jessica Parker, Kirsten
Dunst, Kate Hudson, Gwyneth Paltrow, Helena
Christensen and Jennifer Lopez to name but a few.

Despite such glamorous support, Williamson
has modestly said that he feels that he hasn't
quite made it to the big league of fashion yet.
However this seems only to add to his cult status.

Williamson has a staff of twelve and runs
his modest empire from a four-storey central
London town house. In terms of brand
extensions, he has his own fragrance and
a small lifestyle range that includes scented
candles. In addition, there are plans for to open
a store in spring 2004 in London. But this is
nowhere near enough for this ambitious designer
– Williamson admits that he wants it all –
branded bags, sunglasses, jewellery, shows,
huge advertising campaigns, the works.

Williamson comes from Manchester but
studied fashion at Central St Martin's in London.
He founded his company in August 1996 with
his business partner Joseph Velosa and showed
his first womenswear collection, 'Electric Angels',
during London Fashion Week in September
1997. Bias-cut dresses and separates in tangerine,

fuchsia and magenta were shown on models including Kate Moss, Helena Christensen and Jade Jagger. The fun, vibrant and glamorous clothes made the front pages of British newspapers, as well as getting Williamson's name into French, Italian and American Vogue.

While the press coverage of each of Williamson's collections has been consistently strong, the clothes continue to be commercially viable and are now stocked by over 100 stores worldwide. Furthermore, Williamson now shows his womenswear collections during New York Fashion Week.

One of Williamson's first celebrity fans was Jade Jagger, who wrote to congratulate him on a skirt she had worn for a Tatler shoot. Williamson quickly wrote back to enlist her support. These days they are firm friends, and Jagger was among the celebrities who posed in his clothes for a series of photographs marking his fifth year in business.

Williamson combines colour, texture and pattern to simply "make women feel good" as he puts it. Familiar characteristics of Matthew Williamson pieces are a sense of modernity with exotic colouring and intricate detailing. The aim is to make the wearer feel special, feminine and uplifted. There is also a touch of gypsy elegance, bohemian chic and even hippy-chick about Williamson's clothes: the neon pink dress that Jade Jagger wears in the anniversary photo shoot is based on some fabric he found on a stall in India, and he regularly works with Rajasthani embroiderers.

Without the advertising budget of a Chanel or a Gucci (as of yet) he relies a great deal on his natural charisma to attract PR coverage. Slight, slender and good-looking, Williamson has already been seen in a number of newspapers and magazines draped in his trademark vivid colours with many a beautiful friend.

matthewwilliamson.co.uk

MOËT

Champagne's iconic brand

Ever since its creation in 1743, the House of Moët & Chandon (pronounce Mo-ette) has been associated with status and celebrity: from Louis XIV, one of its first customers to Madame de Pompadour who famously said "Champagne is the only wine that leaves a woman beautiful after drinking". In 1893, Moët was awarded the Royal Warrant by Queen Victoria. In continuing the long-held Royal Warrant, Cuvee Vintage 1942 was released to celebrate Queen Elizabeth II's coronation, followed by Silver and Golden Jubilee cuvées.

Today Moët & Chandon is renowned around the world for its on-going association with the fashion industry. Proud sponsors of London Fashion Week since 1997, followed closely by Milan, New York, Paris, Tokyo, Sydney (and Bombay, Barcelona, Moscow as well), Moët is savoured backstage before and after some of the most illustrious fashion shows. Every season, some 18,000 glasses of Moët quench the thirst of the London fashion scene. Some 70 years after they were the height of fashion in Parisian cafes, Mini Moëts were re-introduced at London Fashion Week, with straws to save models from smudging their lipsticks on glass. Later, in 2002, Moët launched Champagne's first mini bottle of rosé champagne, Mini Moët Rosé, which instantly became the media's favourite tipple. In 1998, the prestigious Moët & Chandon Fashion Tribute was launched to celebrate a designer who has, and continues to, influence the world of fashion both in the UK and internationally. The first Tributee was the glorious doyenne of fashion, Vivienne Westwood. The 2002/03 Tribute was granted to cult milliner Philip Treacy, which gave the fashion gliteratti the opportunity to attend the most lavish party at the V&A museum.

Attended by the likes of Naomi Campbell, Grace Jones, Erin O'Connor, Alexander McQueen, Valentino and Sophie Dahl, the Tribute generated a staggering £2.5 million media coverage and was recognised as 2002's party of the year.

Moët will launch its first concession within London's leading department store, Selfridge's, in the shape of a 70 square meter bar overlooking Louis Vuitton, Dior, Fendi, Celine et al. In 2002 Moët introduced its first 'live' window at Selfridge's that was staged as a backstage scene with models sipping Mini Moët Roses.

In the case of most brands, a vintage collection evokes a museum with rare and beautiful pieces from the past. Moët & Chandon, give today's consumers the opportunity to taste a bit of history with each glass of its vintage champagne. Somewhere underground in their 17.5 mile cellars, you will find some of Moët's finest vintage bottles being stored for future release. Vintage champagne is made exclusively of grapes from a single year, when the harvest has been judged of outstanding quality by the winemaker. Champagne's first Vintage champagne in 1842 was Moët's, and was released to meet the demand from British and American wine lovers for more mature wines. As part of their Vintage campaign, Moët drew upon their collection of archive photography showing glamorous celebrities enjoying Vintage Moët dating back to the 1930s. The Vintage campaign sees the 2003 launch of a glossy magazine titled Vintage, which will feature a wide collection of vintage objects and vintage culture of interest to modern consumers. Moreover, some of Moët's very scarce older vintages (including 1964 and 1978) will be introduced this year for those connoisseurs seeking something even more exclusive, and will be made available in selected Moët Vintage bars in the UK.

moet.com

The Morgan Motor Company is the world's oldest privately-owned motor manufacturer. Founded in 1909, by HFS Morgan, the Company has remained family-run for three generations, with Charles Morgan, HFS Morgan's grandson now at the helm.

The marque made its international debut at the Olympia Motor Show in 1910, with the launch of a 7bhp single-seater three-wheel vehicle. The following year the mark II three-wheeler, complete with two seats, caught the eye of the Harrods Managing Director, which in turn led to the famous store becoming the first-ever Morgan Sales Agent. Nowadays, the sales network has expanded considerably, with a total of more than 60 dealers worldwide.

Morgan is renowned for producing timeless precision-crafted sports cars of traditional style yet contemporary performance. Until recently, it fielded a small core range of models which included the 4/4 – a two-seater model introduced in the 1930s which now holds the record for the world's longest production run of the same model – the 4/4 4-seater and the more powerful 4.0-litre Plus 8, which was introduced in 1968.

However, in 2000, Geneva Motor Show audiences were stunned by the launch of the first all-new Morgan for 60 years, the Aero 8. The brainchild of Charles Morgan himself, this revolutionary aluminium intensive 286bhp sports car was created with a combination of cutting-edge technology and traditional hand-crafting.

To enable the build of such an innovative design, Morgan invested substantially in state-of-the art technology

The first and last of the real sports cars

and a new purpose-built production facility. Such improvements aided the manufacturing process to the extent that the now infamous waiting time for vehicles has been significantly reduced to just twelve months in most cases.

Morgan has also enjoyed an illustrious history in motor racing. In fact, all Morgan models on the road today were born on the race track. The Company believes that sustaining the ardours of racing and rallying is key to producing true sports cars that are powerful yet ultimately reliable.

Morgan's racing history goes back to 1912, when a Morgan three-wheeler won the International Cyclecar race at Brooklands. That same year, the Company's founding father, HFS Morgan broke the 1100cc one-hour record travelling at an average of just under 60mph and this was closely followed by a win at the French Grand Prix at Amiens in 1913.

Throughout the decades, Morgan's racing success has continued at a variety of levels from cross-country rallying to sprint and endurance racing. Morgan even formed its very own Sports Car Championships in 1987 to encourage owners to take to the track.

After a lull in the 1990s, Morgan returned to international racing with the launch of the Aero 8 GTN. For the first time since 1962, when a Morgan Plus 4 won the 2.0-litre class, the Morgan marque returned to la Sarthe for the Le Mans 24-hour race. The Aero 8 challenged the might of Porsche and Ferrari and stayed on track for eighteen hours, outlasting a number of more high profile teams.

That result, in the face of adversity, has prompted a renewed fervour for racing within the Company and a will to bring Morgan back to the higher echelons of the motor racing world.

Throughout its history, the core qualities that have built this awe-inspiring marque – care, craftsmanship and appreciation of the individual – have remained constant and true to HFS Morgan's vision. Time has not stood still for Morgan though. Major technological advancement and product development has ensured that Morgan has kept up with the times, whilst also retaining its identity. More than 90 years on, Morgan has never been stronger and it continues to receive worldwide acclaim for its unique character, traditional values and pioneering spirit.

The Morgan legend lives on…

MUSIC TELEVISION®

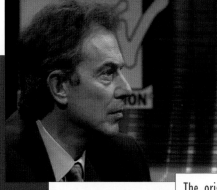

The originators of music TV

Vanity Fair says its logo is "one of the most instantly identifiable on the planet". The Sunday Times says it catapulted Ozzy Osbourne onto the list of richest Britons; Tony Blair has debated international politics on it and it's regularly name-checked by Eminem in his singles. If all the world's a stage, then MTV's is the biggest stadium of them all.

MTV: Music Television was, and remains, the original music television channel. Launched in 1981 by a group of enthusiasts, it has grown into a global brand of epic proportions. From low-key beginnings it's now

Brand Spanking New Music Week

in association with **HMV** top dog for music dvd games

MONDAY 24TH MARCH
THE CARDIGANS THE DONNAS
TUESDAY 25TH MARCH
CHRISTINA AGUILERA
TERRI WALKER
WEDNESDAY 26TH MARCH
MOLOKO THE THRILLS
THURSDAY 27TH MARCH
MELANIE C TRIPLE 8
FRIDAY 28TH MARCH
BLUR AUDIO BULLYS

Catch these exclusive gigs every night at 7pm only on MTV. Starts Monday 24th March.
MTV's Brand Spanking New Music Week brings you exclusive new live sessions recorded at the MTV studios from five of the biggest names in music plus five of the hottest bands tipped for greatness in 2003

✳ EXCLUSIVE TO HMV
WIN A TRIP TO NEW YORK AND VISIT THE MTV STUDIOS!

available in 377 million homes in 166 countries and is known everywhere in the world.

But despite its size, one of the keys to MTV's success is to offer the small, local picture alongside the global. What people want in Athens won't be the same as those in Huddersfield, so the MTV viewers tune in to features content specifically and locally for them. There will always be the Madonnas and JLos who cross international borders, but MTV also makes sure that, British audiences see bands of British interest.

mtv.co.uk

On MTV UK & Ireland, for instance, there is tailor-made programming like Brand Spanking New Music Week, with home-grown bands like Blur and The Thrills performing alongside international stars like Christina Aguilera.

Another of MTV's strenghts is its ability to stage the world's largest music events. Its annual awards ceremonies like the MTV Europe Music Awards boast performances from the cream of music's A List and are watched by a billion people each. Rival UK ceremonies genuinely bear no comparison.

Ground-breaking shows have always been MTV's forte, from the original Big Brother 'The Real World' back in 1992, to Beavis & Butthead, Celebrity Deathmatch and the recent phenomena of Jackass and The Osbournes. Shows like these get the whole world talking. When The Osbournes launched in 2002, the career of Ozzy Osbourne hit a new, unexpected purple patch and the Osbournes became the most talked about family on the planet. MTV UK recently made the cult show Dirty Sanchez, now being discussed in pubs across the land, and in 2003 MTV UK & Ireland doubled its investment in programming to ensure that it keeps entertaining and surprising the public. 2003 also saw the launch of MTV's pioneering new interactive service Peep which gave viewers behind the scenes access to Justin Timberlake's London gig. MTV has also opened up the channel to emerging film makers through its pro-social, 'licence to create' initiatives.

Although for many years it was a lone voice in the world of music TV, MTV started a digital TV revolution. In the UK there are now five MTV channels, plus VH1, VH1 classic and The Music Factory that make up the network. Following in MTV's innovative footsteps is a plethora of derivative music channels, featuring back-to-back videos. In fact, the UK digital viewer can now surf between a staggering 21 music channels 24 hours a day. Will MTV crumple in the face of so much competition? Will it ****, as Ozzy might say.

With 22 years' experience, annual events that grab headlines around the world, seminal 'water-cooler' programmes, enviable relationships with both the biggest and the newest music stars, and greater investment than ever before with which to create TV hits of the future, MTV is most definitely here for the long term.

MUJI
無印良品

Muji's pared-down, stylish products range from clothes and stationary to furniture and kitchen equipment. Inexpensive, practical yet elegant, Muji captures the imagination.

The brand dates back to 1980 and has its roots in Japan. The company was originally known as Mujirushi Ryohin, which literally translates as 'no label quality goods'. The Ryohin Keikaku Company was founded in 1989 to market the concept worldwide, trading in Europe under the simplified name Muji.

The four criteria of the concept are value for money, functional design, understated colours and a full lifestyle range. Packaging is kept simple and uniform, and to prevent wastage Muji

inspects and re-inspects its products at every stage of the production process. The brand believes that products should speak for themselves — what you see is what you get.

The opening of the first Muji shop in London in 1991 marked the European launch of what became an acclaimed retail concept. It was described in the press as everything from "Japan's hottest export" (Daily Mail) to "A kinda funky Marks & Spencer" (The Face). Today, there are sixteen Muji stores in the UK.

As it neared the tenth anniversary of its European launch, Muji embarked on a new stage of its development in the region. As well as expanding on the merchandise available from Japan, it began to develop products specifically for the European market. The first result, the Muji Europe autumn/winter fashion collection, was launched in September 2001 to media

acclaim and strong sales. This was followed in 2002 by the launch of the first Muji Europe household accessories range.

In keeping with its low-profile marketing strategy, Muji's fame has sprung largely from press and public relations, and word-of-mouth. It also sponsors design awards in Japan and the UK. Not surprisingly, over the last decade the brand itself has won a raft of design and innovation prizes.

One of the keys to Muji's success has been its Japanese advisory board, set up in 1980 at the birth of the brand. The board's members are leading names in design fields ranging from fashion to graphics and interiors and includes fashion designer Yohji Yamamoto. They play a crucial role in the brand's overall direction, merchandising policy and marketing strategy. The brand's customers also have a say in product development through its Japanese website, MujiNet. So far, three products have been developed in direct consultation with consumers, with nine more to follow.

Worldwide, Muji continues to go from strength to strength. In Japan, there are 265 stores in total, with recent developments include the opening of a 3,000 square metre flagship store in Tokyo's Yurakucho district. In 2002 Muji revamped its offering in Hong Kong, continuing this strategy

良品大賞'95　　　　作品募集

あなたの良品は人類の良品かもしれない。

in Singapore the following year. On the European front, in 2002 it opened its first franchised store in Dublin, and launched its UK website, muji.co.uk.

In April 2003 Muji Japan exhibited in Milan for the first time, reflecting its policy of encouraging designer collaboration on an international scale. However, simplicity and value for money will remain key. As design journalist Stephen Bayley commented in The Times Magazine in 2001: "Muji is the ordinary thing done extraordinarily well."

muji.co.uk

OAKLEY

Disgust. No one ever imagined a seven-letter word could launch a technology company that would later earn more than 600 patents worldwide. Add contempt, and you've got the makings of an icon that would one day invent the performance tools of professional athletes. Mix in some loathing and revulsion, and the result is a primordial soup that would ultimately produce innovations with enough art to be honoured as a luxury brand, and enough science to be embraced by those whose lives depend on their gear.

Nearly three decades ago, a mad scientist was busy at work in his garage. He despised the term 'industry standard' because he knew the industry had tunnel vision. Conventional thinking disgusted him, and he vowed to defy it. He became dedicated – some would say beyond reason – to a singular purpose: find opportunity, solve with technology, and wrap in art. The year was 1975 and the man was Jim Jannard, an inventor who started Oakley with $300. Today he is a billionaire.

It all began with a motocross handgrip. Jannard reinvented it with an ergonomic shape to better fit the rider's hand. The innovation gained a cult following when Jannard unleashed it on the BMX market. That's when the Oakley founder began work on another invention, a sport goggle that offered superior clarity and impact resistance. Soon the stars of Motocross and BMX were wearing the Oakley icon. In the 1980s, the Oakley O Frame® goggle evolved into athletic eyewear called Eyeshade and Blade. More breakthroughs led to the ultimate in performance technology, a single-lens sports shield known as the Pro M Frame®.

An original, unexpected and innovative world brand

Oakley's defiance of convention has bled from niche sports to pro competition, from BMX rider Stephen Murray and snowboarder Terje Haakonsen to Formula One driver Juan Pablo Montoya. Jannard's pursuit of perfection is inspired every time professional athletes choose to wear Oakley equipment in competition, not because they're paid to do so, but because it pays to do so.

Oakley offers performance eyewear, footwear, apparel, accessories, watches and prescription eyewear to consumers in more than 70 countries around the world. Every invention begins in the company's design bunker, a fortress in California where lasers bombard tanks of acrylic fluid to form 3-D prototypes. CAD/CAM engineering combines state-of-the-art materials in a place that would give a mad scientist nightmares. A few years ago, Oakley was toying with 425,000 watts of plasma

DEDICATED TO PURPOSE BEYOND REASON

oakley.com

lightning when a six-ton generator accidentally blasted through a detonation containment bunker and took out a forklift. The cutting edge is not for the timid.

In the July 2002 edition of Forbes Global magazine, Oakley was ranked in the top 30 luxury brands. It shared the honour with companies ranging from BMW to Prada. But luxury status is just one facet of Oakley's art and science. When the US Elite Special Forces needed footwear for assault missions, they came to Oakley. Their lives depend on their gear, and there can be no greater compliment to a company's dedication to performance technology.

With technologies that range from active sports gear to military hardware, Oakley has tapped into a synergy that radiates with consumers. It's all about making the best products on the planet by letting invention lead the way. Convention is a straightjacket that was shed long ago. Today, the brand's scientists are bent on shattering the limits of possibility.

PROUD GALLERIES

Stunning exposure

Alex Proud had what could be described as an eclectic career before setting up his phenomenally successful private photography galleries. He started out as an antique dealer when he was only 23 years old. The following year found him opening his first gallery, Proud Oriental, specialising in oriental art. He later capitalised on his business by selling bullet proof Rolls Royces to the Russian mafia. After that, like many ambitious young men of the time, he launched himself as an internet pioneer, setting up one of the first auction sites.

But it was with Proud Galleries that Alex really flourished. Launched in 1998, the venture adopted a winning formula of exhibiting accessible shows around popular themes such as music, fashion, film and sport. Whether you want a photo of Frank Sinatra, The Clash, Rankin or Audrey Hepburn, this is the place to find it. It is now said to be Europe's most popular privately funded photography gallery, attracting around 100,000 visitors a year.

With sites in both Central London and Camden, Proud aims to appeal to the upper end of the mass market. The 14-18 shows a year are an entertaining blend of the cult and the legendary. Landmark exhibitions include Destroy: The Sex Pistols; Rankin's Nudes; The Rock'n'Roll Years; Rebel Life: Bob Marley; Underexposed and Hip Hop Immortals.

Press coverage adds up to an advertising equivalent of more than £1 million per exhibition, not least because the galleries have become famous for their star-studded opening nights. Like the brand itself, these parties are as relaxed and fun as they are stylish, with the crowd seeming to barely notice the paparazzi and TV crews surrounding them. Proud has been referred to as the hippest, coolest and most important photographic gallery in newspapers as varied as

THE INDEPENDENT ON SUNDAY

The Sunday Review

1 SEPTEMBER 2002

Reel danger: Robert Fisk
on the battle for Kabul's
film industry

White-hot winter jerseys

Our sizzling guide to the
greatest British bangers

For those about to rock

The Rolling Stones' early years: exclusive
photographs by Gered Mankowitz, plus
eye-witness accounts from the front row

The Sun, the Mirror, The Times and The Guardian. Coverage to date includes over 50 front covers and almost 1,000 features.

Proud has exhibited many of the world's great photographers, and is fast becoming the venue of choice when the hottest talents want to exhibit their latest work. It has also become a sponsorship magnet, raising over £400,000 in 2002 from clients such as Audi, Jaguar, Davidoff and Budweiser.

As its portfolio of shows and international profile has increased, Proud Galleries has started to take its most popular exhibitions on tour. Proud shows have cropped up in galleries from Amsterdam to Tokyo, by way of Melbourne, Paris and Tel Aviv.

Proud has also just strengthened its team by appointing Carrie Neely as its new Associate Director. Carrie has had six years experience in Sales Management in the Art and Photography print market and more recently managed eyestorm's London and New York Galleries.

And what of young Alex Proud? Since 1998, the director and owner of Proud Galleries has become a leading commentator on photographic and media matters, sitting on the panels of various photographic bodies, including the Nikon Press Awards and the Observer Hodge Awards. He has also been asked to create a gallery for the Brazilian Ambassador to London. Vision On, the publishing company he set up in 1999 with the photographer Rankin, has put out a wide range of cult photography books, from The Art of Barbie to the Dazed & Confused Annual. Alex Proud has appeared in various documentaries and is a regular guest commenter on BBC London Live. Not only that, but he was voted one of the country's 100 most eligible bachelors by Tatler. He plans to open two more UK galleries in 2004, and to expand internationally within the next few years.

proud.co.uk

In 1948, Rudolf Dassler founded PUMA from the remains of his family's shoe business in Herzogenaurach, Germany. The early decades were very much about sport, about running shoes and football boots featuring the now globally recognised 'form stripe', about Olympic champions from Tommy Smith to Heike Dreschler, and about football legends from Pele to Maradona.

Through the 1970s the leaping Cat logo of the basketball and tennis ranges became synonymous with urban cool – a mark that immediately identified its wearer as an individual with a particular attitude about both life and sport.

In the 1980s however, as the global sportswear market began to accelerate and transform itself into a world of hyper-marketing, massive athlete endorsement contracts and 'logo-as-design', the brand went through a process of re-organisation. A crowded marketplace was beginning to consume smaller players, and it began to look as though PUMA was destined for obscurity. Like so many other brands that have long since gone, PUMA suffered from consumer saturation – every player in the marketplace was competing to be exactly the same as everyone else. The brand therefore looked for ways to change its fate. "Yes, we're a sports brand, but what else?" was the question that had to be answered.

PUMA had to become more than it had been in its past. After taking a close look at what the brand had been good at, examining the changing marketplace, and looking closely at the attitudes of its core consumers, it became clear that PUMA

was far from what might be considered a traditional sportswear company. For years, the brand had delivered a dual proposition – performance as well as lifestyle. Taking the lead from its own audience, listening to what consumers were saying with their behaviour, the brand defined itself in both ways, and began to 'mix things up'. No individual is one-dimensional, interested in only sport or only fashion. It was therefore concluded that PUMA's brand personality should likewise never be limited. The definition of a new category, 'sportlifestyle' was born.

However, this transition was not an easy undertaking. For years, growth was slow, and challenges were numerous. But as an understanding of 'mixing it up' developed within the company things began to click. By the late 1990s the comeback was fully underway, typified by new ways of thinking about PUMA and the marketplace – partnerships with musicians and artists, the return of heritage shoe styles, development of sport-fashion collections – all were PUMA firsts.

As market share grew and the logo began to reappear as an underground alternative to the typical offerings of an overheated sports market, things began to really take off – new advertising, new websites, new retail stores in key cities around the globe, and a new understanding of the way consumers react to the brand. The leaping Cat became an icon of the underground – a symbol for the 'alternative' to the norm.

'Mixing things up', continues to drive the brand into new territory. Recent innovations include a 26 piece modular fashion menswear wardrobe for the global business gypsies called '96 hours'. The collection steps away from pure sportswear and includes everything that one would need in 96 hours of business travel. Furthermore, it all fits in a simple aluminium case. Meanwhile, Puma's Nuala line of yoga-inspired clothing has been designed in co-operation with Christy Turlington – seamlessly blending fashion with performance. In addition, modern approaches to sport trainers have led to the development of Mostro and Speed Cat.

For PUMA, the definition and ownership of the new sportlifestyle category is simply the reflection of its own consumers, and they wouldn't want it any other way.

puma.com

RAYMOND WEIL
GENEVE

It is said that the first two things people look at when they want to know how much you're really worth are your shoes and your watch. By sporting a RAYMOND WEIL timepiece one's chance of exuding opulence is greatly improved.

Raymond Weil, who gave his name to the brand, was born in Geneva in 1926 and joined one of the city's watch firms in 1949. Having always admired the technical qualities of beautiful timepieces, he quickly worked his way to the top. In 1976, after 27 years in the watch trade, and at the height of the crisis within the Swiss watch industry, Weil decided to form his own company. At the beginning he travelled the world like an itinerant salesman, with his models in his pockets. But it was not long before buyers recognised Weil's passion and craftsmanship. The company now has an international distributor network covering 86 countries. Much of it based on relationships that were established 25 years ago.

A crucial moment in the watch manufacturer's history came when Weil retired and his son in law, Olivier Bernheim, became his successor. Bernheim joined the company in 1982 after starting his career as a sales executive with Kronenbourg and later moving to Unilever. This experience with multinationals proved useful when he joined RAYMOND WEIL, which was expanding fast but wanted to retain the mentality of a family business. Bernheim steered the company through this delicate period, taking firm control of its communications strategy. He became President and CEO in 1996.

The RAYMOND WEIL philosophy has always been one of creation, innovation and evolution. Although its products are divided into five collections, its flagship is Parsifal, which the company regards as the pinnacle of its brand, representing the very best in Swiss watch making. Its distinguishing features are clean, symmetrical lines softened by elegantly rounded edges. The dials are protected by sapphire crystal glass. The bi-colour version comes with a mother-of-pearl dial and diamond dot markers, and it also has a diamond bezel.

To reflect this kind of craftsmanship, RAYMOND WEIL advertising campaigns have often focused on themes like 'movement' and 'precision', as well as underlining its commitment to music and the arts. The most recent campaign took 'simplicity' as its theme, but added a winking reference to show business. It showed the watch in a single spotlight, as if on stage. The print campaign was backed up with point of sale material showing RAYMOND WEIL sponsorship activities and celebrity endorsements.

Unlike many luxury brands, this watchmaker has no plans to move into other product areas. Even its logo has changed little over the years, underlining the status of RAYMOND WEIL as one of the last independent Swiss watchmakers, and an understated icon.

The links that have been forged with RAYMOND WEIL and the arts, or more specifically with music, are reflected in the names of the watches themselves. Operatic associations are used for the time pieces Parsifal and Don Giovanni, with broader musical themes like Tango and Chorus employed elsewhere in the RAYMOND WEIL collection. In addition, the brand has been connected with a wide range of musical events and organisations, from a party for the record label BMG to music charity Nordoff-Robbins. The most recent winner of the RAYMOND WEIL Prize for music students was the classical pianist Chi-Ming Shui. Elsewhere RAYMOND WEIL has been involved with popular classics babes Bond, and enjoyed celebrity endorsements from the likes of Samantha Mumba. The brand is also a corporate partner of the Royal Opera House and sponsors its Season Guide, ensuring that it remains true to its classical roots.

RAYMOND WEIL
GENEVE

www.raymond-weil.com

time to celebrate

raymondweil.com

Parsifal
Steel and 18K gold
sapphire crystal
water resistant

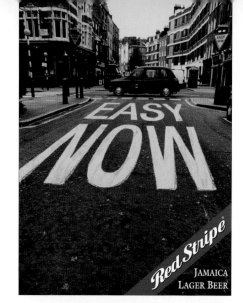

One super chilled,
well travelled Jamaican

With its roots in Jamaica, it is no surprise that Red Stripe has a laid back, easy going personality. However it may be more of a revelation to find that the Red Stripe name is thought to have been inspired by the stripes on the trousers of Jamaica's policemen.

The brand was conceived by Eugene Desnoes and Thomas Hargreaves Geddes after they first met in the office of the West Indies Mineral & Table Water Company, in Kingston, Jamaica nearly 100 years ago. The two men had the same vision in mind – to build a brewery to produce Jamaican beer of international quality. Their determination paid off and in 1927 Desnoes and Geddes announced the opening of the Surrey Brewery on Pechon Street in the heart of downtown Kingston, Jamaica. Little did the pair imagine that they would be destined to brew one of the world's most distinctive, famous and finest premium lagers, let alone create a 'cool brand'. Furthermore, the birth of Red Stripe was later considered to be a milestone in Jamaica's history.

In 1976 Charles Wells Ltd, established in the UK in 1876, became the first brewer outside Jamaica to be granted a long-term agreement with Desnoes & Geddes to brew, package and distribute Red Stripe. A close check is kept on the production of the product to ensure that the Red Stripe one would find in London is the same as the Red Stripe found in Jamaica. The same yeast and hops are imported from Washington State's Yakima Valley and used to ensure that the distinctive taste and easy drinkability is maintained.

To reinforce Red Stripe's contemporary edge, Red Stripe has forged strong associations with surf culture and fashion. It is now the official sponsor of the British Surfing Association and is the named sponsor at the Red Stripe British Longboard Championships. Furthermore, Red Stripe is currently touring the UK's universities and colleges with the surfboard equivalent of a mechanical bucking bronco. Those who manage to stay on board can collect their surfing picture from the Red Stripe website.

Meanwhile, the brand continues its strong association with the music scene — another natural accompaniment to chilling out. Red Stripe has a longstanding association with live music and sponsors a wide variety of events throughout the year. These include The Big Chill, at Eastnor Castle in Herefordshire, in August. Red Stripe is also present at Jamaica's Reggae Sumfest — a major festival featuring acclaimed stars from R&B, Hip Hop, Reggae and dance. Another important event is Wakestock — Europe's wakeboarding and music festival, held in Abersoch, North Wales.

Red Stripe is also a keen supporter of 'Carnival' and is ever present at Europe's biggest street party, the annual Notting Hill Carnival in London.

2003 heralds a number of significant developments for Red Stripe, including new improvements to the can's packaging, which aims to reflect the vibrancy of the brand. There has also been a new creative approach to the brand's advertising, which blends humour with the need to chill out whilst underlining Red Stripe's Jamaican heritage. Furthermore, there is a new look website that reflects Red Stripe's affinity with the urban scene.

redstripe.net

RUBY & MILLIE

Ruby and Millie, both self confessed make up obsessives, developed this brand using their expert knowledge and experience. Indeed, it was highly inevitable that Ruby, a world renowned make-up artist who's created looks for the world's top photographers and most influential fashion designers, including John Galliano, Jasper Conran and Ghost would have her own cosmetics line one day. It was more than fortunate that Millie, an internationally successful beauty publicist who has worked with brands like Aveda and Shu Uemura, should market the concept.

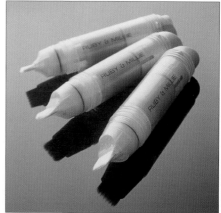

The duo were originally approached by Boots to work on a beauty project which developed into the Ruby & Millie brand. After two years of development, the brand was unveiled in the UK in 1998 using Harvey Nichols department stores in London and Leeds as their launch pad. The brand was subsequently rolled out at larger Boots stores nationwide. Ruby & Millie proved to be immensely popular which led to the brand facing rapid expansion. In the UK it doubled the number of outlets by the end of 2000. The same year saw the publication of 'Face Up', Ruby & Millie's first beauty book which coincided with the launch of their accessories range available in 400 stores.

Ruby & Millie has been hailed as one of the most innovative brands to be launched in the international beauty sector for decades. It brings together the experience of two beauty industry professionals Ruby Hammer and Millie Kendal who, over a period of two years, lovingly created a range of almost 300 products. Each item has been approved by both women to form a collection that not only Ruby and Millie want to wear, but are confident that their friends, mothers, grandmothers and children would want to wear.

The Ruby & Millie philosophy is to create beauty that is achievable and affordable, enabling all women to accentuate their natural beautiful and feel glamorous and gorgeous.

It is sophisticated yet simple; experimental yet accessible; and above all, fun. These values extend throughout the brand. Its packaging, co-designed by Wright & Teague, has

been designed using a combination of mirrored and transparent materials to echo the individual's identity while reflecting the brand's integrity. It has been imitated by many mainstream brands, and has become a stable entity in the application and design of modern cosmetics.

Another key element of the brand is the environment in which it is sold. Its in-store boutiques were designed by Hosker, Moore & Kent with the aim of being a playground for women to have fun and experiment. Hard sell techniques and complex makeovers are abandoned in favour of the concept of an in-store Make-up Advisor. The idea being that this gives friendly advice that women really want with solutions to their specific problems. The advisors treat the work area as a dressing table and use the mirror to show customers how to apply their make-up, using their own face as a canvas of experimentation.

As Ruby and Millie have said, "Ruby & Millie is for the individual, who aspires to being strong yet demure, professional yet sexy, young yet mature. It's all about the freedom to choose who you want to be today."

Power and performance reinforced by safety and innovation with no superficiality in sight

The bold lines of a Saab readily set the car apart from others on the road. The brand's distinctive approach to design is much more than skin deep – combining originality and flair with excellent performance has been the basis of this brand for over 50 years.

The first Saab rolled off the production line at Trolhattan in Sweden half a century ago.

Conceived by aeronautical engineers unrestricted by conventional automotive design wisdom, those early cars set the distinctive Saab design theme which characterises the brand.

In today's automotive market that is becoming ever more homogenised, Saab's individuality has stood it in good stead. The brand is established as a significant player in the UK premium car sector with a comprehensive product line-up embracing sporting saloon, estate and convertible models. Saab often sets the pace across a range of key areas: design, safety, driving pleasure, performance, technical innovation and concern for the environment. Its cars aim to reflect an individual statement combining flair with common-sense, enjoyment and satisfaction with safety and security. These key elements are communicated in its adverting which is always refined and sophisticated.

Engine performance is paramount with Saab's reputation founded on innovation and its expertise in turbo charging technology. Furthermore, it was the first manufacturer to put a turbocharged car into volume production. Compared to their competitors all Saab cars offer more power and performance per pound. Saab's turbo charged cars can generate smooth pulling power instantaneously at any engine speed ensuring swift and secure overtaking which minimises risk exposure.

Saab has also introduced direct ignition and on-board engine software, which is in fact more powerful than that used in the Apollo space capsules which have put men on the moon.

Saab has always wanted its customers to enjoy driving. Motoring pleasure and satisfaction is manifest in a number of ways. The design and comfort of seats for example is an industry benchmark. Models were fitted with heated front seats more than 30 years ago, well ahead of the trend, while interior air filters were introduced in 1978. Saab took the comfort revolution one step further with the new Saab 9-5 by becoming the first car manufacturer to install ventilated front seats. Furthermore, both the new 9-5 and 9-3 models, feature the world's first interactive head restraints – an important step in minimising whiplash neck injuries.

Technical innovation also extends into other areas of safety and Saab is also recognised as an industry leader in this field. Its cars are among the safest on the road and all surpass the most stringent international requirements governing passive safety, the ability of a car and its passengers to survive a crash intact. Saab was fitting side-impact bars and energy absorbing bumpers to all its models in 1972, well ahead of the rest of the industry.

The brand's hallmark front wheel drive on all models gives safe, secure handling and excellent grip in the rain. Saab was an industry pioneer when it fitted diagonally-split dual brakes some 40 years ago, while head lamp wash/wipers were fitted more than twenty years ago. In 1991 the company became the first automobile manufacturer in the UK to equip as standard all models with anti-lock brakes.

As with road safety, environmental concern is very much part of Swedish culture and is fully expressed in the design of Saab cars. The company was first to fit asbestos-free brake pads and has eliminated harmful CFCs from all products.

All told, this is one very reassuring brand.

saab.com

Scalextric has captured the imagination of pre-teens for generations. Recently it has been benefiting from the rise in popularity of Formula One, which makes up a significant collectors' market. However, the trend amongst adults, the majority of which are male, to rekindle memories of their youth with Scalextric is many fold. This has come about due to a leaning towards unpretentious brands that show honest, clear credentials. Furthermore, it is now perfectly acceptable for adults to be hooked on video and computer games, which were previously pastimes reserved for children only.

Due to its popularity, Scalextric has been transferred into a large-scale format for adult parties and as after dinner entertainment. The current system allows for tracks of up to eight lanes to be designed allowing multiple drivers to race at the same time, with a computerised start and timing system (the Race Management System) keeping the races in order.

The Scalextric brand, which is now owned by Hornby, was originally developed by a company called Minimodels who began producing clockwork cars under the name Scalex in 1952. By the late 1950s this evolved into a track-based electric system and the brand became Scalextric. In the late 1960s the launch of a banked figure-of-eight circuit was a turning point for the brand, as it immediately proved popular. In addition, cars became even more detailed – up to the point of printing insignia directly onto the bodies, rather than using transfers.

Now Scalextric is the pre-eminent name in slot car racing, aided by its continuing focus on accuracy. Cars are often based on the original prototypes of the vehicles that inspired them, with Computer Aided Design replicating even the tiniest details.

The Sport Advanced Track System, launched in 2002, was the first major change to the track in over 40 years. It is flatter, smoother, quicker to assemble and has a deeper slot – combating the familiar problem of cars sailing off the track. New cars made specifically for the system feature ground axles and brass bearings to create smoother running and an even better grip.

Scalextric is soon to launch an intelligent 'pacer car system' for the new Scalextric Sport era which it calls The Challenger System. It represents the toughest challenge to solo drivers Scalextric has ever issued. Based on the new Mercedes CLK DTM, the on-board Challenger micro computer allows the car to learn any circuit and then race it to the optimum.

Scalextric continually develops its cars to keep up with what is happening in the real world. For example, the new BMW Mini Cooper and an Italian Job licensed set were developed to tie in with the big release of the Hollywood remake which hits screens in September 2003.

For the 2003 Le Mans 24 Hour Race Scalextric have produced a replica of the TVR T440R which will take part in the race. Other new models include US Indy Racing League cars.

Scalextric has become a sponsor of the Goodwood Festival of Speed, which takes place annually in July. To mark the occasion a limited edition three car boxed set of the 1966 Le Mans 1-2-3 finishing Ford GT40s have been produced.

Scalextric has survived a lot of competition in its time, but the thrill of racing still generates excitement and sparks players' competitive streaks.

scalextric.com

SCRABBLE®

WHEN FRANK BEAT SARAHS BOTTOM WITH DANDELIONS GEOFF STUFFED THEM BOTH WITH GORGONZOLA

SCRABBLE
EVERY WORD COUNTS

THRASH YOUR BOYFRIEND WITH ZUCCHINI

SCRABBLE
EVERY WORD COUNTS

WHERE ELSE CAN YOU GET POINTS FOR FARTING

SCRABBLE
EVERY WORD COUNTS

A mind-sharpening war of words

Poughkeepsie in New York State was in the depths of depression in 1931, like the rest of the US, and local architect Alfred Butts found himself out of work. With time on his hands and a natural interest in words and games, Butts began to develop a game which he called 'Lexico'. Played without a board, players scored on the basis of the length of the words formed. In the late 1930s he came up with the concept of combining letters with a board, allowing words to be joined, but the game was still commercially unsuccessful.

After World War II Butts joined forces with Jim Brunot, a government social worker who believed it was possible to market the game. Together they refined the concept, rearranging the premium squares and simplifying the rules. They then lodged a copyright application, which was granted on December 1st 1948 and the name SCRABBLE® was registered fifteen days later.

Brunot, who became a driving force for the game, worked from his living room and assembled 2,250 games by hand in the first year. The real break came in 1952 when Jack Strauss, Chairman of Macy's became addicted to SCRABBLE when introduced to the game by friends on holiday. He subsequently placed a large order for the game and initiated a major promotional campaign for his world famous department store in New York.

SCRABBLE captured the imagination of thousands of Americans and by the following year 6,000 sets were being produced per week.

The game's popularity spread as far afield as Australia and was also launched in the UK by J W Spear & Sons where the game became an instant success. In its first year, 4.5 million sets were sold worldwide. Over 100 million games have now been sold in 121 countries around the world and SCRABBLE is currently produced in 30 different languages.

The brand is now available in a wide range of formats including PC CD ROM and internet versions as well as Braille, Pocket Magnetic, Deluxe and Junior editions to name but a few variants. Other SCRABBLE initiatives include TV Scrabble on Challenge TV plus the World Scrabble Championships.

SCRABBLE now has something of a celebrity following with the likes of Jonathan Ross, Jo Brand and Carol Vorderman flexing their vocabulary with the game. Furthermore, couples such as Brad Pitt and Jennifer Aniston, Gwyneth Paltrow and Chris Martin from Coldplay also play. In addition, the sexy pop goddess Kylie Minogue plays SCRABBLE in between touring, while other players from the music scene range from Boy George to Damon and Alex from Blur.

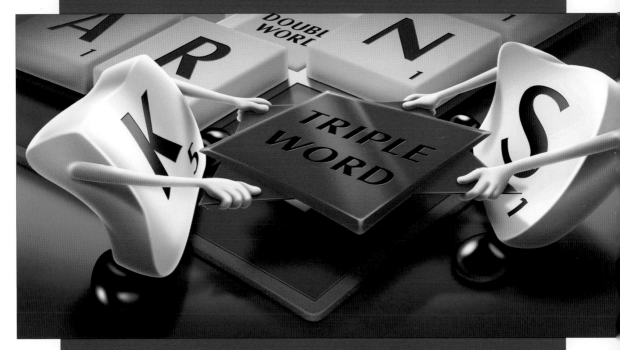

The diverse list of star players continues with Keanu Reeves, Queen Elizabeth II, Michael Jackson, Richard Branson, Linda Evangelista and Coolio all being keen players of the game.

SCRABBLE has sealed a place in the nations hearts with its strong heritage, but has also won the respect of trend setting urbanites with its natural, unpretentious and honest values.

scrabble.com

SELFRIDGES&C°

Selfridges is the ultimate retail experience brand, where as much thought is put into what happens in the store as to what's sold in it

Selfridges' inspiration today comes from its founder Gordon Selfridge, the US entrepreneur who in 1909 left his job at the famous Chicago retailer Marshall Fields to launch his own business in England. Selfridge saw the department store as the centre at the heart of urban life – a microcosm of a major city offering myriad experiences to an eclectic mix of people. Accessibility was key.

In keeping with the founder's vision, Selfridges has plans to create an additional 100,000 square feet of retail space in Oxford Street as well as adding a contemporary hotel, restaurant and car park. What's more, the brand is becoming more accessible to trend-hungry urbanites outside London. By the end of 2004 Selfridges will have four stores, including the new Birmingham store, two stores in Manchester and the famous Oxford Street store. In the next few years Selfridges plans to open a further four stores in locations such as Newcastle, Bristol and Glasgow.

Selfridges today sells over one million products and is packed with the world's most creative designer brands. None of these products could be described as necessities for living: more as extras to make life better. While the store appeals to customers because of these products, the secret of Selfridges' impact as a brand is that it places as much importance on what happens inside and outside its stores as to what is sold inside them.

So even before entering the stores the innovative window displays – designed by the in house marketing team, who in 2003 have worked with Rankin, Britart and Walter van Bierendonck – give you an idea of what lies inside.

The importance placed on the visual impact of Selfridges' stores has been taken to the extreme in the design of the new store in Birmingham, that opened in early September 2003. Voted number five in The Observer's preview of the most important cultural events to happen in the UK in 2003, this building redefines the way that customers experience

SELFRIDGES&Co
body craze
MAY 7th-31st

brands. Designed by architects Future Systems –
who shot to fame with their design of the media
centre at Lords cricket ground – Selfridges'
Birmingham store is a completely curvaceous
structure, covered in 15,000 spun aluminium
disks with no traditional shop windows or
external branding.

But this pursuit of the most amazing shopping
experience doesn't stop at the shops themselves.
Selfridges has tried to bring an equal amount of
intuition and innovation to the major promotions
staged within the stores, creating pure retail theatre
that attracts the attention of both customers
and the media.

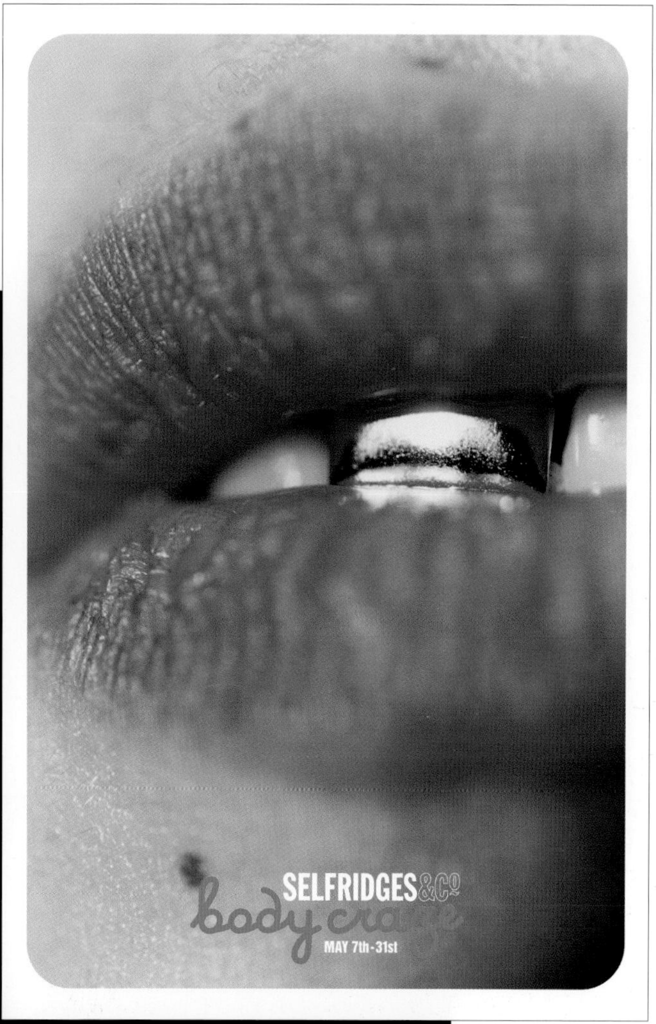

These promotions include Selfridges' 'Body
Craze' in 2003, a month-long celebration of our
fascination of the human body in all its diversity. Throughout May, Selfridges'
three stores were given over to an enormous variety of live events and
installations from performers and artists such as Acrobat Productions,
Random Dance, Walter van Bierendonck, Rankin, Cees Krijnen, John
Kamakazi and Spencer Tunick.

This followed the success of '23 1/2 days of Bollywood' in May 2002,
the biggest celebration ever of Bollywood's film culture with over 60 live
events as well as appearances by Bollywood star name Amitabh Bahchan,
Dimple Kapadia, Madhuri Dixit and Hritik Roshan.

To set the seal on its success, in 2002 Selfridges won the Glamour
magazine award for the most Glamorous Department Store and in 2003
won the Retail Week award for the In Store Promotion of the Year for
'23 1/2 days of Bollywood'.

selfridges.co.uk

SHISEIDO

Shiseido was Japan's first western style pharmacy and is now one of the world's oldest (as well as fourth largest) cosmetics companies. The brand has always prided itself on being highly innovative and combining pioneering research with strong design.

The Japanese pharmacist Arinobu Fukuhara, founded Shiseido in 1872 to create total well-being for the body and mind through innovative cosmetic solutions combining 'Eastern esprit and Western science'. The brand's early clientele included royalty and the elite of Tokyo society. The Shiseido range has grown over the past century to include skincare, body and haircare, suncare, make-up as well as fragrances.

Design and packaging has always been considered as important to the Shiseido brand as the product itself. In 1916, Arinobu Fukuhara's son, Shinzo set up Shiseido's first in-house design department. He was a well travelled and talented art photographer and spearheaded design and advertising that hadn't been seen in Japan before. Shinzo gathered together the best artists of the time and created Art Nouveau-inspired posters and advertisements.

In the 1930s ads showed an idealised, new, self-assured woman and boldly combined western and eastern influences. Shiseido's artistic heritage progressed with the brand's internationalisation in the 1960s. Photography was used to reflect changing times and create a modern feel. The 1980s saw the appointment of the French artist, Serge Lutens, as the brand's 'international image creator'. Lutens was responsible for establishing Shiseido's personality in Europe as well as creating the colour palettes of the company's make-up ranges.

Product packaging has also been held in high regard. In the early days a sense of elegance was established with distinctive arabesque graphics incorporated.

Such attention to detail continued and can, for example, be seen in the asymmetric form of the pure perfume bottle for Féminité du Bois. Based on the female form, the bottle, launched in 1992, is finished by hand so that no two are the same.

The other side of Shiseido's character is its pioneering technological innovations. These have included aromachology research, which began in 1984 to investigate the physical and psychological effects of scent on the mind and body.

Shiseido works with scientists at its research centres around the world using pioneering bio-technological solutions. It has also founded the Cutaneous Biology Research Centre with Massachusetts General Hospital and Harvard Medical School.

Shiseido offers its customers the opportunity to learn the truth about their skin and see visual proof of the efficacy of its products. The 'Multi Micro Sensor' machine takes a magnified image of the customer's skin before and six weeks after they start to use their suggested skincare.

In 2001 Shiseido launched its first new makeup collection in twelve years, called Shiseido The Makeup. World famous makeup artist Tom Pécheux was appointed as the 'colour creator' and also collaborated with Mario Testino on the advertising campaign.

Shiseido's product portfolio comprises some of the most innovative solutions to modern skincare concerns. In October 2002 Shiseido launched Future Solution Total Revitalizing Cream. Working at a genetic level, the cream enables mature skin to perform at the optimum level and produce more of the vital components that keep it looking youthful.

Furthermore, 2003 sees the UK launch of the revolutionary Body Creator Aromatic gel. It is based on Shiseido's groundbreaking proven Slimming Theory, which illustrates how a gel containing caffeine and an aromachology fragrance is able to affect the body's metabolism and enable the break down and burning off of fat. Body Creator was Shiseido's best selling product in 2002, selling one bottle every 3.75 seconds in its first month of launch in Japan alone.

shiseido.co.uk

◑ smart

open your mind.

Innovative, fun and stylish

The love child of watch manufacturer Swatch and car manufacturer Mercedes-Benz, smart's name comes from Swatch + Mercedes + Art, and has been the UK's most successful new car launched in the last twenty years.

The two brands both began thinking about the possibility of a car specially designed for city use some years ago. Swatch first began considering launching a city-car in the 1980s, while Mercedes Benz' original city-car plans which were hatched in the 1970s were put on hold. In 1994, the two companies came together to create MCC (Micro Compact Car), and smart was eventually unveiled to the world in Frankfurt in 1997, with the Europe-wide launch taking place in 1998. The same year, DaimlerChrysler took a 100% stake of MCC.

Launching to the British public just two years ago, the UK has become the third biggest market (behind Germany and Italy and equal to France – all of whom have been established two years longer), with a 98% growth rate in the second year. Globally (smart is in 23 countries, from France to Croatia and Japan), sales grew six-fold between 1998 and 2001.

With a belief in taking the brand to the consumer rather than waiting for them to make contact, events and roadshows allow people to climb in, explore and experience the smart concept.

Fun to drive and easy to fall in love with, this economical, easy-to-park runabout is a truly non-demographic product and has no typical customer. smart city-coupé drivers range from 18-80, while owners range from lovers of micro cars and two-seaters to style fanatics and urbanites.

However, interest has not just come from private sales, as business customers including pizza delivery companies and the emergency services have shown a keen interest in owning a fleet which has lower CO_2 emissions than any other petrol vehicle on the road. Furthermore, it is efficient and nippy about town and its changeable body panels not only offer simple customisation options but can be quickly and cheaply replaced individually.

smart's can also be ordered online. You are invited to design and build your chosen smart on the website, then order the car from your nearest smart retailer. And the smart customer loyalty pledge doesn't stop there. Buy one of these babies and you subscribe to a lifestyle, which includes discounts on everything from parking to ferry travel and car hire.

smart has already won some prestigious industry and customer satisfaction awards, including the Top Gear Awards 2000 Style Award, Auto Express New Car Honours 2002 and Best City Car, and Top Gear Magazine's Motoring Survey 2002, coming top in the city car and ownership costs categories, second best manufacturer and third best car overall (out of 120 models). Along with a stylish new brand icon, 2003 sees the smart brand getting ready to welcome a new family member – the roadster. It is lower and longer than the original smart and is more a sports car. Even before its launch it is proving to be popular and already has a 1,100-strong waiting list of eager buyers. Looking ahead to 2004, the launch of the forfour (four-seater) model, will see another step in the evolution of smart.

thesmart.co.uk

SOS 'SMITHS' OF SMITHFIELD

Prime quality, choice cuts; dedicated to the Best of British, food supplied from independent farmers; people who understand real food

'Smiths' of Smithfield (SOS) is a four-floor restaurant in a Grade II* listed building in the heart of Smithfield Market, London. Headed up by John Torode, SOS opened in 2000, dedicated to sourcing and serving the 'Best of British' (BOB) produce in a friendly and a relaxed atmosphere.

Each of the four floors has a distinct style – food, design and atmosphere – offering pretty much something for everyone depending on mood, budget or time, but each sits comfortably under the 'Smiths' of Smithfield umbrella brand. The overall aim? To be accessible, egalitarian, but most of all a place to relax and have fun.

The Ground Floor Café opens at 7.00am – serving big all day breakfasts and market specials till 5.00pm, thereafter the booze takes over until closing – often accompanied by DJs.

The First Floor Bar is open every evening serving classic cocktails and some new 'Smiths' favourites alongside a small bites menu. In addition, the newly remodelled Private Room has its own bar, cloakroom and kitchen.

'Smiths' of Smithfield Dining Room on the second floor is flooded with natural light from the huge windows on either side of the restaurant. Steaks, big burgers, whole grilled fish, lucky squid are just some of the favourites that are served. And finally, the Top Floor Restaurant. In many respects considered the icing on the cake, a long, clean room dedicated to (amongst other things) serving the best of British Rare Breed steaks in London. The Top Floor also has a wide outside terrace, which is open during the summer with stunning views across the market, the City and St Paul's.

In addition to the restaurant there is now also the outside catering arm – SOS OUT, as well as Lickleyhead Castle – a castle in Scotland with seven bedrooms which is available for hire either catered or not.

The Smiths brand was born from collaboration between the original shareholders and a team comprising Gabriel Murray, Mark Harper and Rodney Fitch. The brand represents everything that the restaurant stands for; the building, the interior; the food; the atmosphere; the staff and the customers.

The identity very much represents Smithfield as a whole. The boldness of the text font, colour and language taken from the market, the traders and the signs dating back to the 1900s meaning that it quickly integrated itself into the vicinity whilst creating its own values. It has derived strength from the consistency of its application. It is not an identity that is based on current design trends, instead it has a timeless classic quality which in turn makes it a design classic.

Over the years the brand has been nurtured and developed by John Torode in conjunction with Mark Harper who have always held a strong belief that the only way to court success is by staying true to the core business. As a rule Smiths never advertises, rarely self-promotes and always seeks to reach existing and new customers in a quirky way. Valentines Day 2003 saw a number of key 'Smiths' clients and journalists receiving a 12oz vacuum packed steak encouraging them to 'get stuck into some rump'.

The development of own-brand 'BOB' beer (British Organic Beer/Best of British) has further strengthened the Smiths brand whilst showing a willingness to evolve and play with identity. The beer designs have been nominated for numerous awards.

Excellence, passion and loyalty are at the heart of 'Smiths' – it has recently been succinctly summed up by the Thames & Hudson 'Style London' book as 'a new London institution'.

smithsofsmithfield.co.uk

SONY

From TVs to headphones, camcorders to radios and everywhere in-between, Sony's reputation for powerfully slick design married with progressive technology precedes it.

Sony was founded in 1946 by Akio Morita and Masaru Ibuka, who started out repairing radios, but soon began designing their own products. By the 1950s, it had already developed a reputation for innovative hi-tech design through products such as the first Japanese tape recorder, the first efficient transistor radio, and the first all-transistor television. It rapidly expanded into neighbouring Asian markets as well as the US and Europe.

Sony continued to notch up pioneering inventions, from the first colour videocassette recorder in 1971 to the famous WALKMAN personal Hi-Fi in 1979. The latter, initially dismissed as a gimmick by critics, became the biggest selling consumer electronics product in history. When the WALKMAN became an essential fashion accessory in the 1980s, no one could foresee that some twenty years later the cassette format would sit alongside so many other formats. Sony developed the next generation of music format with the CD player and then the CD WALKMAN. It has continued to research new formats such as the MiniDisc. However, Sony has also developed in the home entertainment market with vast and ever advancing product ranges including TV, video, DVD and Hi-Fi formats — not forgetting the mighty PlayStation.

Sony has also brought its expertise to computing through brands such as the VAIO Notebooks and Desktops as well as CLIÉ Handhelds, whilst providing professional audio-visual and IT equipment as well as its range of mobile phones.

Sony has driven our ever more sophisticated 'digital lifestyle' with the latest technological innovations focusing on the need of 'connectivity' — the convergence

between home entertainment and computing. Needless to say, the latest generation WALKMAN is unrecognisable from its predecessors – with its evolving sleek, compact design it can store many hours' worth of music.

This ability to identify and act on consumer and industry trends has served Sony well over the years. It was arguably the first global electronics corporation to recognise the importance of synergy – the interface between hardware and content. It bought CBS Records in 1988 and Columbia Pictures Entertainment a year later, becoming a powerhouse in the global entertainment industry. Sony Music Entertainment's roster includes the likes of Oasis, Shakira, Jamiroquai and Michael Jackson, as well as jazz and classical performers like Wynton Marsalis and Herbert Von Karajan. On the movie front, Sony Pictures Entertainment is behind blockbusters like Terminator 3 and Charlie's Angels: Full Throttle.

Sony carefully nourishes its personality, through careful marketing. Its strategy is to support the brand throughout the year, rather than just at peak times such as the run up to Christmas. Sony's marketing has often been as innovative as its products. For instance, when the WALKMAN was first launched in Japan, employees were encouraged to stroll the streets of Tokyo listening to the new product, creating a valuable buzz. This generated huge media attention and so much demand that Sony's entire stock was sold out within three months. More recently, when it launched MiniDisc in the UK, Sony targeted bars and clubs with postcard drops. And in 2002, to promote the 'Go Create' concept, Sony UK launched the Go Create Experience, an interactive roadshow that allowed consumers to get their hands on Vaio laptops, digital camcorders, Network WALKMAN and other new products. Its intelligent electronic dog, AIBO, also became the star of Sony's ads to give the brand a more accessible face.

The company's latest advertising uses the line 'Products for People', reflecting its position of making technology more human, and putting cutting-edge science in the hands of ordinary consumers. The campaigns emphasise that without involving people, technology has no value.

sony.co.uk

Four of the world's most stylish galleries for showcasing the best of International and British art from 1500 to 2003

Tate Modern opened in May 2000 with a dramatic nocturnal launch televised by the BBC. London's first national museum for modern art is housed in the former Bankside Power Station.

The famous Turbine Hall, running the whole length of the vast building, now makes a breathtaking entrance. At the top of the building is a new two storey glass structure which provides natural light into the upper galleries, and houses a café offering outstanding views across London. Tate Modern's collection spans from 1900 to the present day, and includes works by Dalí, Picasso, Matisse, Rothko and Warhol as well as contemporary artists such as Bill Viola, Gilbert & George and Louise Bourgeois.

It's now three years since the gallery opened and over thirteen million people have visited, confirming its position as one of the leading cultural attractions in the world.

The original Tate Gallery was renamed Tate Britain in 2000 and focuses on British art from 1500 to the present day. It's housed in Tate's original nineteenth century building a few miles further west on the Thames at Millbank. The Collection presents an unrivalled picture of the development of art in Britain including the magnificent Turner collection. The opening of the major Centenary Development in 2001

TATE BRITAIN

DAYS LIKE THESE

Tate Triennial
Exhibition of
Contemporary
British Art 2003

Admission free
26 February – 26 May

Tate Britain
London SW1
⊖ Pimlico
www.tate.org.uk

In partnership with Volkswagen
for Phaeton and Touareg

tate.org.uk

has created more space to showcase British art as well as a dramatic new entrance on Atterbury Street.

The new Tate to Tate boat service has made it easy to travel between Tate Britain and Tate Modern. It runs daily during gallery hours and also stops at the British Airways London Eye.

Tate's out-of-London galleries in Liverpool and St Ives (Cornwall) opened in 1988 and 1993 respectively. Tate Liverpool is located in a converted warehouse in the city's Albert Dock, whilst Tate St Ives makes the most of the legendary Cornish coastal light with its beachfront position. Both present art selected from the Tate Collection and special exhibitions of contemporary art loaned from other public and private collections.

It was the splitting of the London Tate Gallery into two that stimulated the creation of a new identity. In March 2000 a new logo, a Tate font and a colour palette symbolising openness, change and vision were unveiled. This coincided with the launch of the award-winning website, new staff uniforms designed by Paul Smith and new signage at all four galleries.

The launch of Tate Modern and Tate Britain was accompanied by a high-impact advertising campaign which communicated the spirit and values of the new Tate through adverts which used the strapline 'Look Again, Think Again'. As well as collaborating with The Guardian (the media partner for the launch of both galleries, and a key collaborator today), Tate has developed partnerships with a broad range of brands including wagamama, Kirin Beer, Selfridges and the Royal Mail.

Research has shown that international awareness of both Tate Modern and Tate Britain has continued to rise, with a growth of 18% between 2000 and 2001. In addition, Tate Modern has become the most popular modern art gallery in the world, as well as the third most popular tourist attraction in Britain.

teatro

Slickly blending discreet exclusivity with opulence and comfort

Opened in February 1998 to critical acclaim, Teatro has positioned itself as a style-leader and a calm, mobile free oasis from the hustle and bustle of London's West End and the glare of the paparazzi flashbulb. Teatro is an intimate and discreet retreat with what The Guardian described as 'squashy black leather furniture and dark wood detail'. Members can visit throughout the day for a quiet drink, tête-à-tête, business meeting or meal.

Teatro oozes exclusivity. It has been designed to provide successful people, and those in the public eye, with a discreet, sophisticated haven away from their busy lives. The exclusive private members club's ambiance changes throughout the day. In the daytime it offers a peaceful environment to conduct everything from breakfast meetings to lazy lunches and pre-theatre drinks and in the evening takes on a more lively atmosphere with great tunes which never compete with conversation.

Teatro exercises a strict policy in order to ensure its members have maximum privacy when relaxing in the comfort of a secure and private space. No cameras or mobile phones are permitted and Teatro never discloses the presence of its high profile members to the press. That is why Teatro's has some of the leading lights in the world of the arts and business amongst its members. Teatro membership is billed as a 'lifestyle choice' and members have additional benefits via access to a wide range of lifestyle management services. The Concierge Service offers a booking service for members – everything from train and theatre tickets to hair appointments and gym recommendations.

Teatro is the brainchild of husband and wife team, ex-footballer Lee Chapman and actress Leslie Ash. The couple sought to create a tranquil and sophisticated environment which their friends and colleagues would enjoy.

They planned a modern, affordable restaurant coupled with an exclusive private members club. To establish the most comfortable environment, they called upon the talents of

teatrosoho.co.uk

an award-winning design team already noted for their work for The Clarence Hotel, Dublin, and the Metropolitan Hotel in Mayfair, which includes Nobu and The Met Bar.

In the exotic 'East meets West' environment of Teatro's public bar and restaurant SO.UK SO.HO, one has the opportunity to drink, dine and lounge in Teatro's famously relaxed yet opulent surroundings.

To accommodate the general move away from fine dinning restaurants, and the demand for more atmospheric and relaxed dining, Teatro closed its public restaurant and launched SO.UK SO.HO in April 2003. Designed by Martin Brudnizki and his team, who created the critically acclaimed Daphnes in Barbados, the venue has an exotic, eastern theme with mystical Buddha figures, rich fabrics and informal low level seating around engraved brass Moroccan tables. The menu consists of killer cocktails and designer Asian Fusion dishes. Progressive French dance with North African beats, are the main focus of the music the DJ plays nightly from 10.30pm.

Quite simply, Teatro offers the perfectly located and non intrusive canvas for its members and restaurant guests to relax, socialise, entertain and be entertained until the early hours. Teatro boasts nothing other than it's dedication to offering un-compromised service, some of London's best cocktails along with quality, fresh and most of all delicious food.

TOPSHOP

A fashion emporium that blends cutting-edge style with affordability

Described by model Liberty Ross as "just the best thing ever" and loved by fashion addicts, models and celebrities alike. Topshop has evolved into a fashion label that exemplifies up-to-the-minute affordable style.

Topshop was born in 1964 as a department store concession in Sheffield and grew to become a mediocre high-street store. That was until it was transformed into an achingly modish retail outlet, which attracts 180,000 visitors each week – including the likes of Kate Moss, Helena Christensen, Mis-Teeq, Kelly Osbourne, Liv Tyler and Gywneth Paltrow. There is also growing demand for Topshop abroad – particularly among the jet set of New York.

Key pieces now fly off the rails within minutes, and during last September's London Fashion Week, some members of the international press skipped catwalk shows to go shopping there.

The driving force behind the transformation is Brand Director Jane Shepherdson, who has been rated as one of the most influential people in fashion of her time. Along with her team of buyers and designers, gut instincts are followed to introduce elements that they feel are right for the brand. This is a concept that is obviously paying dividends – with 285 stores in the UK and a further 59 elsewhere in the world.

One key ingredient in the brand's success has been its vision of shopping as entertainment – the 85,000 square-foot flagship Oxford Circus store (the world's largest fashion store) has its own TV and radio station, nail bar, Topshop Cafe, live performances and in-store events.

Recently made over from shabby chic to stark and contemporary by design duo Shumon Basar and Joshua Bolchover, Topshop Boutique houses Topshop's designer collections, and features one-off handmade pieces by the store's in-house label, Unique. Its launches create a whirlwind of excitement by pushing the boundaries of fashion. Alongside this, the TS Design label features designers including Sophia Kokosalaki and Hamish Morrow.

The British Fashion Council's 'Retailer of the Year' since 2001 and the biggest supporter of young fashion designers in the UK, Topshop's annual sponsorship programmes include Graduate Fashion Week, the Re:Creation creativity awards and the British Fashion Council's New Generation Award. For the latter, fifteen up-and-coming designers are given financial support to showcase their autumn/winter 2003/04 collections at London Fashion Week.

Industry awards are numerous, and include The Face magazine's Best Place to Shop, Best High Street Retailer (The Independent), Most Glamorous Place to Shop on the High Street (Glamour Awards 2001) and Best Shop to Splurge £1000 (In Style Celebrity Shopping Awards 2002).

On a mission to create the ultimate shopping experience, Topshop has come up with a menu of extra services set to transform the way you view shopping on the high street – Style Advisor is a personal shopper who's on hand to help the style hungry get the best out of a shopping trip, handpicking the cream of the season's looks and dishing out honest advice. Chosen because of their flair for service, the team of advisors were put through their paces by industry leaders, including the fashion editor of Dazed and Confused. The free, no-obligation service includes access to the VIP fitting room, complimentary refreshments and a fast-track payment service which is now available in 30 stores nationwide.

October 2002 saw the redesign of the Topshop website by cutting edge agency, Hi-res making it the number one fashion destination online. With over 120,000 newsletter subscribers www.topshop.co.uk features up to 100 new styles each week.

topshop.co.uk

A seductive, chic yet classic icon

Not only is the Vespa one of the world's most enduring symbols of cool, but it has reached this status from humble beginnings. The fact that its appeal has withstood the changing fads and fashions of nearly 60 years adds weight to its iconic stature.

The legend of Vespa was born in 1946 from Enrico Piaggio's vision to meet post-war Italy's urgent need for modern affordable transport. Corradino D'Ascanio, an aeronautical engineer who designed and constructed the first modern helicopter, was given the job of designing a simple, robust vehicle which could be driven by both men and women, would not dirty its rider's clothes, and which could also carry a passenger.

The scooter was designed to be affordable and functional, a vehicle for the masses which would get Italy moving again after World War II. Ironically, the very design features which made it so practical – the 'step-through' seating position, the simple mechanics, the metal body – are now fundamental to its personality, and are the foundations upon which the scooter industry has been built. Yet, few scooters can claim to come close to Vespa in terms of image, status or appreciation.

The Vespa first gained worldwide recognition when screen icons Audrey Hepburn and Gregory Peck weaved through the streets of Rome on one in the 1953 film Roman Holiday. After years of austerity, the 1950s saw a new exuberance start to emerge, and the sight of two young lovers astride a Vespa in a city of romance captured the hearts of millions. When the Vespa was adopted by the Mods some years later, the thrill had a harder edge, a hint of danger and rebellion. These very different influences combined with the innate Italian-ness of the Vespa created the stylish image to which so many aspire. As Italian author, Umberto Eco, said, "The Vespa came to be linked in my eyes with transgression, sin and temptation."

More than 100 different models of Vespa have been produced, and over sixteen million have been sold since 1946, each with the distinctive look and feel which set this scooter apart from others. Whether a classic machine or the latest Vespa Granturismo 2003, the curve of the body, the angle of the wing mirrors, the shape of the headlight are always inimitably Vespa. And on the front shield, the logo which is recognised and admired the world over.

The Vespa logo is in itself a design classic, and now can be found on clothing and accessories enabling everyone to buy into the Vespa legend. The brand ensures that everything which bears the logo must be of the same high quality, with a style combining practicality and beauty, with a touch of that indefinable essence of Vespa.

Much of Vespa's marketing is about being in the right place at the right time, being seen with the right people and associating with the right brands. These relationships include customisations by the likes of Salvador Dali, Agent Provocateur and Dolce & Gabbana; events and exhibitions; dozens of films featuring the Vespa and celebrities through the ages extolling the virtues of the Vespa.

The fact that the Vespa has featured in many of the most famous museums in the world, including The Guggenheim, The Design Museum and Le Centre Georges Pompidou, is testimony to its place in design and automotive history. Indeed, there is now a Vespa Museum in Pontedera, Italy, where the scooter's heritage can be traced through the years.

From its inception 57 years ago, the Vespa has remained true to the original legend and design heritage. One look and you can tell it's a Vespa.

vespa.com

vitra.

In a post-Wallpaper world, where an increasing number of consumers are turning away from traditional furniture stores and seeking designs that are both beautiful and inventive, Vitra is a name to be reckoned with. Its entire raison d'être is to create furniture that makes homes and workspaces ergonomically effective, healthy, creative and inspiring.

When Willi Fehlbaum founded Vitra in Switzerland in 1950, it was a shop fitting company. Later it moved into manufacturing office chairs, and its fortunes changed for good in the late 1950s, when Fehlbaum met the now-iconic designers Charles & Ray Eames and George Nelson. He obtained permission to produce their designs under licence for the European market. Another landmark came in 1977 when Willi Fehlbaum's son, Rolf, took over as chairman. That same year, Vitra launched its Vitramat chair, with an advanced synchronised movement developed and patented by the company.

Over the years, Vitra has developed a reputation for aesthetic purity and the high quality of its designs. Its most famous advertising campaign, called 'Personalities', focuses purely on its design heritage, showing famous people – from Audrey Hepburn to Linford Christie – perched on their favourite Vitra chairs. Even the brand's logo, which was designed by Pierre Mendell, has the timeless simplicity of its furniture.

Joyn designed by Ronan and Erwan Bouroullec, photographed by Miro Zagnoli.

vitra.com

After a fire at its factory in Weil am Rhein, Germany, in 1981, the company decided to rebuild the site as a showcase for contemporary architects. This was the beginning of the Vitra Architectural Park, which includes buildings by Nicholas Grimshaw, Frank Gehry, Tadao Ando, Alvaro Siza and Zaha Hadid. In this way, the company's headquarters reinforces the brand's reputation for technical excellence and creates an inspiring strong visual impact, defining what Vitra is all about. Needless to say, its employees work in an environment entirely furnished by Vitra products, which reflects its belief in the importance of a healthy and inspiring workspace.

Following the same logic, the Vitra Design Museum was created in 1989. It houses a huge collection of chairs, both historic and modern, and curates exhibitions held in the museum at Weil am Rhein, before touring internationally.

Vitra has produced designs that have become modern classics, including Maarten Van Severen's MVS Chaise, Jasper Morrison's Ply chair and Antonia Citterio's Visavis chair. Products like the Ypsilon chair, with its external supporting frame, flexible 'sail' backrest and the extended reclining position, underline Vitra's commitment to innovation.

And the tradition continues: in 2002 Vitra launched a re-edition of Jean Prouvé's furniture designs, and has recently bought a Prouvé garage which will be added to the architectural park in Weil am Rhein. It has also launched a new office system called Joyn, designed by the Parisian brothers Ronan and Erwan Bouroullec. Based on a simple French farmhouse table – which can accommodate numerous activities – it is practical, economical and fun. The designers used the concept of 'throwing away the screwdriver' to define their creation, because it can be adapted for myriad purposes without the need for tools.

Vitra's designs have won countless awards, including plaudits at the FX International Design Awards for three years in a row. From the 1950s to the present day, Vitra has been at the forefront of design – leaving others without a leg to stand on.

The new Volkswagen Beetle has been widely appreciated as one of the trendiest cars on the road ever since it was first unveiled, to great excitement, in 1996. People have never stopped loving the 'bug' and Volkswagen's careful re-interpretation of the design classic draws on Beetle's strong heritage to create a quirky, evocative and ultra-modern car that is unmistakably a Beetle.

Now, Volkswagen is paying tribute to another legend – the Beetle Cabriolet. The original convertible Beetle, which dates back to 1949, quickly became one of the most popular and successful cabriolets on the road, with an enduring cool factor which makes them a collectors' item – and command high prices – even today.

Now, the New Beetle Cabriolet is set to repeat the feat of its predecessor and become motoring's latest fashion icon. Unveiled at the Detroit Motor Show in January 2003 and on sale in the UK since April 2003, it is already an award winner. It was selected by 'What Car?' magazine as being the 'Best Cabriolet of the Year' for 2003.

The New Beetle Cabriolet retains many of the design quirks of the original. It has the pram-like hood, which sticks out behind the rear seats when down. This might look messy on many modern convertibles, where the roof folds into a hidden compartment, but it seems exactly right on this, complementing the New Beetle's curvy lines and helping the model keep that old-world charm and quirky sense of fun.

As with every other element of the car's design, the retro-look of the hood doesn't mean it compromises on meeting modern expectations. It takes just thirteen seconds to open or close, has a sophisticated sealing system to keep wind noise down at speed, and is easily controlled by a single latch.

A fun loving, curvy and quirky individual

The New Beetle Cabriolet.

Photography by Nick Meek

The New Beetle Cabriolet. VW

Illustration by Ian Bilbey (C.I.A)

Like its predecessor, the new model also gives its occupants a real 'open air' feeling, achieved by positioning the windscreen further forwards and offsetting the front seats slightly towards the centre. Compared to many modern cabrios, which compromise on 'upwards freedom' because of large windscreen frames and roll bars, the New Beetle Cabriolet has a particularly generous amount of roof-free space – perfect for the sun-loving, style-appreciating motorist.

But this extra freedom has not been achieved by sacrificing safety. Volkswagen claims the car is one of the safest open-topped cars on the road, with an advanced roll-over protection system. The system automatically detects if the car is in danger of tipping over and, if necessary, supports extend from behind the back seats in a quarter of a second. The body has also been specially reinforced to provide added rigidity.

Inside, the car retains the saloon version's ultra-cool cabin, with retro styling. A few design tweaks have been made, such as a re-working of the centre console to accommodate an optional CD system. After all, good tunes are an essential element of open-top driving.

Available in four models, with 1.6 litre or 2.0 litre engines, the New Beetle Cabriolet is generously equipped with ABS anti-lock brakes, driver and passenger airbags a sophisticated alarm system (featuring 'radar' interior protection) and Volkswagen's Electronic Stabilisation Programme.

Beetle has an illustrious advertising history with memorable, innovative and irreverent ads that date back as far as the brand itself. The ads for the New Beetle Cabriolet again reflect the brand's loveable, individualistic personality in a familiarly charming way.

But the main thing about this car is that it is undeniably, achingly, beautifully, stylish. It's a guaranteed head-turner and looks set to follow in the footsteps of its revered parent in becoming a twenty first century design classic.

wagamama

Japanese style and design have been popular influences on many elements of Western culture for some time now. With regard to food, noodle bars and sushi restaurants are now an increasingly popular feature on UK high streets.

The key element to good Japanese food is its freshness and healthiness. When this is combined with restaurants that are clean, minimalist – distinctively Japanese in design the formula is very strong.

The essence of wagamama is a no-nonsense combination: simple, high quality yet inexpensive food served up in a sleek, minimalist canteen-style setting, with bench seats alongside an open-plan kitchen. Together these all contribute to the noisy, vibrant, buzz of the restaurants.

wagamama has had regular queues outside its doors week after week since it opened its first noodle bar in 1992 in a London backstreet, near the British Museum. wagamama now has a total of 22 restaurants which includes sixteen in and around London and three in other cities around the UK including Manchester, Nottingham and Bristol. Further afield, wagamama has franchises in Dublin, Amsterdam and Sydney. There are also plans to open further branches in the near future both in the UK and internationally.

Much can be learned about wagamama by examining the meaning of the name itself. Translated literally from Japanese, wagamama means 'wilful/selfish child'. But a broader interpretation would explain the selfishness in terms of looking after oneself, in terms of positive eating and positive living. A single-minded belief in its principles and letting the quality of its product speak for itself, has built wagamama into an extremely strong and much admired brand, as well as enhancing its cool credentials.

The personality of wagamama is also very apparent in its uncomplicated advertising. An image that is frequently used in its ads, amongst other communications, is that of an eager diner with a large bowl completely covering her face as she slurps up what is left in the bottom. Shot in black and white, the image gives an air of being both innocent and childlike but confident and wilful at the same time.

wagamama has also won a string of awards, for example at the prestigious Retailers' Retailer of the Year Awards 2002, wagamama received the 'Best Concept' award and was a finalist in the 'Best Design' category. Also in 2002, wagamama won 'Best Restaurant Website' at the caterer.com awards. Furthermore, this is the second year running that the brand has achieved Cool BrandLeader status.

The wagamama personality is conveyed in its unconventional way of doing things. It doesn't get carried away with some of the fuss and ceremony often found in restaurants and focuses on delivering great food at excellent value (average spend is around £11 per head). Orders are taken on the latest technically advanced hand-held electronic devices and zapped straight to the kitchen via radio signal, where each dish is cooked and served immediately. Meanwhile the numbers of the dishes you order are enthusiastically scribbled on your paper placemat by the friendly waiting staff. wagamama is all about going with the flow and if that means a party of people getting their food at different times, or sitting at a bench next to a stranger or even queuing briefly until seats become free, then so be it.

wagamama.com

wagamama and positive eating + positive living are registered trademarks of wagamama ltd.

It's good to play together

Xbox. The word that many a girlfriend dreads. The flip side being an epic adrenaline rush that glues gamers to their sofas right through the night.

The awesome capabilities of Xbox reflect what is now possible in this arena with superior graphics quality, online gaming capabilities, advanced audio output and one of the strongest portfolios of games ever seen.

With a mission to provide the best, most powerful video game experience available, Xbox was first unveiled in January 2001, going onto the US market in November 2001 and becoming the most successful launch of a video games console ever. By the end of December that year, 1.5 million systems had been sold. After an eager wait, Xbox was launched in Europe three months later and saw queues of excited gamers waiting to experience what was being hyped as the biggest console launch ever.

Since its conception, Xbox has been utilising the internet as well as street and youth culture to spread the word, and give games enthusiasts a taste of the Xbox experience. In the run-up to the UK launch, 'Xperience events' were held and sampling pods set up in fashionable bars, record shops and snowboarding and music events. Meanwhile, a controversial 'Life is Short. Play More' TV and cinema advertisement depicting a person's journey through life in just three minutes was banned for being too disturbing, but became cult viewing on the web.

At the 2002 Xbox showcase event X02, the Isla Magica theme park in Seville was transformed for two-days to unveil more than 80 of the world's most wanted new games to European press and retailers. Microsoft also took the opportunity to announce it had purchased UK-based Rare Ltd –

one of the world's leading video game developers. The deal further demonstrated Microsoft's commitment to providing the most innovative interactive experiences available.

Also on show was Xbox Live, the revolutionary online gaming service, which launched in March 2003 in eight European countries. With Xbox Live, players can connect and play great games with people across Europe, the US, Canada and Japan, chatting with friends and meeting new ones to share game experiences online, no matter where they are or what time it is. In North America, where it launched in November 2002, gamers claimed they were spending all their free time gaming. Now there are over 500,000 Xbox Live gamers worldwide, 50,000 of those in Europe. Ibiza was targeted in August 2002, when Xbox invited journalists from the music and style press to play games and party hard. A few months later, a luxury London dockside apartment was transformed into the Xbox Loft and hired out for a two week period to show off the latest in Xbox gaming and a whole host of exclusive games.

In 2003 Xbox seized the opportunity to take the Xbox experience to the slopes with Xbox Big Day Out, a freestyle ski and snowboard competition in Val D'Isere, which is one of the biggest events on the snowboard calendar. Supported by Oakley (another Cool BrandLeader) over 10,000 spectators were estimated to have attended the event. Other events supported included Urban Games, the street style event attracting 25,000 people on Clapham Common and King of Street, the BMX and Skateboard event in Birmingham.

Xbox now has nearly 220 games to choose from and has more than 300 more in the pipeline. There are new eagerly awaited titles like Project Gotham 2, Top Spin and Fable, while Halo 2, which was voted best console game at E3 in May 2003, promises to be one of the most ambitious games ever created. So gamers, put that night out on hold and take your position on the sofa.

xbox.com/uk

Easy.

I mean, we've all been in situations where we've said, 'that's cool'. All spontaneously passed comment on a particular remix, hairstyle, shirt in your granddad's wardrobe, cuddly toy or whatever. But then when you think about it for a minute, 'cool' isn't so easy to explain. It gets all intangible. Which is a bummer when there are a fair few brands around which rely on cool as their principle competitive advantage.

Here's what I think.

Some read 'cool' as 'trendy'. They see 'cool' as sitting ahead of an invisible 'adoption curve' or at the peak of some 'consumer triangle'. They argue that a discrete community can identify 'cool' ahead of the more conservative mainstream. Indeed they go further and posit that this community are sufficiently influential that they can sanction what is cool.

So if 'cool' means 'trendy', making something cool is relatively straightforward. Just get the endorsement of 'Opinion Leaders'.

Except…

Except this isn't really how 'trends' work anymore. The world has sped up. The time between a trend's inception, adoption and disposal is now so quick as to make all talk of 'Opinion Leader foresight' utterly redundant. We are living in a time of culture squash. Take the coolest music producers in the world, The Neptunes. They're just as comfortable, and respected, writing for Busta Rhymes as they are for Britney and Nike ads. Moreover they'll do all three in the same week if you ask them.

So if 'trendy' doesn't mean 'trendy', then cool definitely can't.

And when you think about it – it never did. Sometimes things are cool precisely because they are not at the sharp end of change. Some things are cool because they steadfastly refuse to change. Irrespective of opinion. Muhammed Ali's stance on Vietnam conscription? Pretty cool.

So is it non-conformity then? Is that what it takes to be cool?

Yes.

Sometimes.

And sometimes not. A group of 50 year olds who turn up at Gatecrasher, bedecked in tie-dye and selling herbal ecstasy, are probably not conforming to convention. But God, you wish they would.

So. Not trendy. Not necessarily non-conformist. What then?

Is it about believing in something? About representing that belief? Providing a reference point around which like-minded people can gravitate? Yes. I think this is probably part of it. Most cool things tend to have a fan club.

Moreover history tells us 'cool' can endure in a way that fashion cannot. 'Cool' can be sustained, have depth and substance whereas fashion is necessarily temporary, shallow and superficial. Brands, bands and world leaders who believe in something tend to endure. Those that simply reflect the transitory tastes of 'consumers' become vacuous shells. There's nothing solid within. And that's not cool.

So standing for something help makes you cool.

But I'd argue a couple more things are needed.

Firstly something that future-proofs your 'cool'. That prevents 'cool' from becoming 'cult'. In a word – energy. The energy that drives you on to keep making what you stand for manifest in a series of cool and fresh ways.

And I'd say you need standards in order to be cool. You need the pig-headed determination to do everything as well as it can possibly be done. Keeping standards high is the secret of Dr Dre's enduring cool. And Sony's. And adidas'.

So, for me, three things help make something cool. Belief, energy and standards.

We can decide to fill the world with meaningless, one-off crap. Or we can fill it with a stream of top-notch culturally significant things. Now what would be most cool?

Dylan fluked his way through LSE and into BBH. He then claimed all credit for Levi's, Lynx and Audi before bribing his way to some industry awards and onto the board. Now he's blagged himself another plum job as Planning Chief at Grey. He's a kid. He'll get found out. He's rubbish.

www.grey.co.uk

DYLAN WILLIAMS
Executive Planning Director
Grey London

Defining the x factors that make a brand 'cool' is difficult because cool brands connect with us at a level we don't talk about so easily, particularly in the UK. Cool is about having a deep and rich relationship with the brand, sharing and connecting with values that are important to us as individuals and providing a currency for us to share those values with people who are important to us. People who value our own opinions and whose opinions we value.

While 'cool' is a not a brand descriptor used comfortably by many over the age of 40, cool brands still exist and they have similar roles. Irrespective of our age or language, when we find a cool brand, we tell the people around us. In telling them, we extend the pleasure of our discovery and share an experience that helps us connect with people. If they adopt the brand themselves, the brand becomes evidence of our shared connection and this shared connection breathes further life into the brand's cool status.

But brands that hunt us down are not cool. A cool brand doesn't need to hunt us down because a cool brand is confident we'll find them. Begging for attention is not cool. The secret is in letting people feel they've discovered the brand themselves. Cool brands know that freedom, friendship and honesty are amongst our highest priorities.

So what defines a cool brand is about how they relate to us and how they connect with us; it's an emotional connection. Creating a cool brand requires a very deep understanding of what's important to your target audience. That's much more than simple demographic, behavioural profiling and measuring stated preferences. Brands we think of as 'cool' understand our personal values and they behave in ways that reflect this understanding.

We also expect our cool brands to be consistent. In a world where just about everything can be copied, when we find a brand we really connect with, we want relationship stability. The ability to continually innovate while maintaining an emotive connection provides the surprise-and-delight that's particularly important to 18-35 year olds who are balancing constant change with a desire for connection. Cool designer brands

epitomise this balance and are therefore implicitly as well as explicitly aspirational. Cool brands don't earn their status by simply having the latest or best functionality or design.

Our global annual study into personal values and brand values (Roper Reports Worldwide) yields insights for how one might go about transitioning a cool local brand into a global 'power brand'. Simply put, two types of value differences need to be reconciled. These differences exist between the explicitly cool-conscious 18-35 year olds and older adults and also between UK values and the values of the global or regional community in which we may want to develop our cool brand. The table shows common ground exists on three dimensions; brand fundamentals, how brands make us feel and on one, very key brand value.

Sally Campbell is Director of Brand Strategy at NOP Research Group Europe. A New Zealander by birth, she has also lived and worked in Australia, Hong Kong and New York. At NOP, Sally partners with sector-specialised teams on brand strategy and marketing effectiveness research.

www.nop.co.uk

SALLY CAMPBELL
Director of Brand Strategy
NOP World

NOP World
United Business Media

Common Ground: 'Life Enjoyment', Relationship & Fundamentals

- **Teen Cool Brands:**
  - **Perform**
  - **Are innovative**
  - **Are consistent**

  - **Make teens feel:**
    - Inspired
    - Happy/cheerful
    - Smart
    - Ahead of the pack/like a trendsetter
  - **Share teen values**
    - Excitement
    - *Enjoying Life*
    - Having Fun
    - Friendship
    - Freedom

- **Global Power Brands:**
  - **Perform**
  - **Are innovative**
  - **Are consistent**

  - **Make us feel:**
    - Many things!

  - **We think value:**
    - Creativity
    - Wealth
    - *Enjoying Life*
    - Status
    - Honesty
    - Beauty
    - Power

Source: Roper Reports Worldwide

NOP World

And so we have a simple four-step recipe; balance consistency with innovation, perform as promised, recognise that the relationship is paramount, share an appreciation for enjoying life and the reward is a smooth path to global Power Brand status.

COOL BRANDS ARE THOSE THAT SPOT THE RIGHT TRENDS....AREN'T THEY?
By Phil Teer

As eras go, the end of the 1960s was fairly emphatic: Hell's Angels murdering people at a Rolling Stones gig; the mire of Vietnam; peace demonstrations and race riots – within a short time, all these put paid to Peace and Love.

And into this turmoil, Coke announced that it would 'Like to teach the world to sing.' This branded message promoted the cause of the anti-material 1960s, just as it hijacked that ideal for blatant commercial gain. The fashions and ideas of the hippie 'early adopters' were going mainstream, and Coke was leading the charge.

Many brands comment on the times they're in. Faddy brands live off these times, hoping a cultural wave will carry them for as long as possible. But truly cool brands go further. They don't just reflect the times they are in, they help define them, shaping trends for their target audiences.

Because we do need help in making sense of the world. People sometimes want to be told which side to take – or at least where and what the different sides actually are. Brands can take a stance on our behalf, becoming symbols of what we stand for.

In the 1980s, brands like Porsche and Rolex became more than mere demonstrations of material wealth and success: they were reference points of the age.

When the party ended, the 1990s trends of spiritualism and reflection were apparent in Feng Shui and dressing down. IKEA went from nowhere to market leader by helping build a new open-mindedness, urging us to 'chuck out the chintz' and 'stop being so English'.

But what now? Can brands help us figure out what's going on today? Any anthropologist of the future would be able to look at current ads for male grooming products, breakfast snack bars and supermarket ready meals and get an idea of what's going on in our culture. Ads showing grown men playing practical jokes on each other, or strong women kicking their men out of bed for offering up the wrong 'erotic' ice cream, paint a pretty clear picture.

But these ads aren't necessarily by great brands. They are rarely done by brands we would think of as cool. Mostly, they just reflect trends.

Truly cool brands understand the dynamics of trends. Only in this way can they go further than describing trends and contribute to shaping them. They understand that trends are not just change for change's sake – those are mere fads, idle interest in novelty. Trends are directional, and are in opposition to something. Work is taking up more of our time. Women are asserting their dominance over men. Men are looking for new forms of identity.

Great brands seize trends by the scruff of the neck, create cultural missions, and exhort us to get involved, actively embracing change and taking advantage of it.

A great brand sees an audience increasingly concerned about health, decides that 'anyone with a body can be an athlete', and says 'Just do it'.

A great brand senses that we're increasingly judging our own looks by the same standards we judge celebrities, and tells people 'Remember, life's one big catwalk.'

A great brand recognises the potential we all have to make technology work for us rather than vice versa, and urges us to 'Go create'.

These brands, these ideas, are so successful that they transform businesses. Because in some small way, they change people's lives.

It is harder now. It's a more complex world culturally now than when Coke did this in the 1970. We're more sophisticated, cynical, uncertain and demanding than we were.

But in 30 years time, while we'll find today's combats and Hoxton fins as hilarious as 1970s Coke's kaftans and long hair, we'll still be talking about brands like Sony and Nike, still calling them cool brand leaders because of what they did – because of the way they helped define their times.

Phil Teer worked as a planner at AMV and Chiat/Day before co-founding St. Luke's in 1995, where he has worked on brands such as IKEA, Clark's Shoes, Fox's Biscuits and BT. Phil became Planning Director in 1998 and Joint Managing Director in 2002.

www.stlukes.co.uk

PHIL TEER
Joint Managing Director
St.Luke's

StLUKE'S

CAN A MAINSTREAM BRAND BE COOL?
By Howard Beadle

Cool celebrates its 50th birthday this year. Since Marlon Brando's surly biker king, Johnny, explained what he was rebelling against by demanding, 'What ya got?' back in 1953, cool has become an aspirational mindzone marked by exclusivity, outsidership, irony and the rejection of convention. It has become prevailing generational ideology for 18-35 year olds.

But chasing the mirage of true cool has never been harder. We're all trying to be part of the same club, and logic suggests there isn't room for every one of us.

Can mainstream brands be cool? The old definitions no longer apply. While the margin of cool – expressed by a chase for the hot accessory, 'in' place or hip new band – is dwindling all the time, much larger, mainstreamed strains of cool are emerging. There is a culture building around consumption of things with all the signifiers of cool, but none of the confrontational elements. David Beckham and Justin Timberlake personify this: both are stylish, talented and desperately attractive (like 'The Wild One's Johnny), but neither are radicals challenging the orthodoxy (unlike Johnny).

Much of this directly proceeds from the media boom – through which we get information on the commodity of 'cool' via TV, radio, print, email, text and web – has precipitated an acceleration of uptake from the margins, where cool evolves, into the mainstream. To many, true 'cool' effectively died when establishment figures Tony Blair and Bill Clinton appeared flaunting their rock 'n' roll credentials by playing the guitar and sax in public.

The prism of the media makes stark these changes in the culture. While the style press – once the last word in 'cool' ideas, music and fashion – continues to sell fewer and fewer copies, the circulation of magazines like Heat soars. Justin Timberlake appears on the cover of both The Face and Heat. Which is really 'cool'?

This points to the emergence of a society in which greater education, spending power and taste has made acquisitive consumers of us all, eager to trade up in life through our consumer choices.

For brands, several conclusions arise for from this. Firstly, that attempting to own 'cool' rarely works. Adopting 'cool' language, trends and ideas risks creating a 'groovy dad' syndrome – appearing too eager to solicit approval by affecting a falsely 'cool' manner. Cool generates upwards in culture; it fails to work when imposed downwards.

Secondly, that the acceleration of mainstream uptake from subcultures occurs at such as rate that brands have to move with lightning speed to keep apace.

Some examples subtly balance popularity with mystique and exclusivity. Brands that manage this provide identity, experience and status for the consumer: the true insidership of 'cool'. A consumer's knowledge of what their product or brand choice brings is key and to that extent, brands need to tell an authentic story in an imaginative way to make the transition.

Successful examples include Stüssy, So Solid Crew, Evisu, Hang Ten, Havannna Rum, Radiohead and the US casualwear company, Paul Frank Industries. They made a name with t-shirts and accessories adorned with the company's own cartoon characters, and are now developing an animated cartoon series with those characters in it. Japanese denimwear brand, Evisu, combined a strong heritage with high quality to become a breakabout clothing marque.

Brands need to be able to tell a good story and capture the imagination. Doing so allows the consumer to generate a favourable disposition and decide for themselves. Because, in the end, cool is just a state of mind. It's just one that more and more of us have.

Howard Beale is an ex-journalist with extensive experience in working with well-known brands on a global, regional and local level. He has built partnerships with clients including Motorola, ABSOLUT Vodka, Nike, Microsoft MSN, adidas and KPN/NTT DoCoMo. In 2001, Howard co-founded The Fish Can Sing, an international PR agency. The Fish Can Sing specialises in delivering big, brand ideas that tell an imaginative and relevant news story to build brand reputation.

www.thefishcansing.com

HOWARD BEADLE
Managing Partner
The Fish Can Sing

THEFISHCA
NSING

Agent Provocateur
Agent Provocateur Ltd
18 Mansfield Street
London
W1G 9NW

Alexander McQueen
Alexander McQueen
10 Amwell Street
London
EC1R 1UQ

Asahi
Asahi Beer Europe Ltd
17 Connaught Place
London
W2 2EL

Audi
Audi UK
Yeomans Drive
Blakelands
Milton Keynes
MK14 5AN

Bang & Olufsen
Bang & Olufsen UK Ltd
630 Wharfedale Road
Winnersh
Berkshire
RG41 5TP

Beck's Bier
Scottish Courage
Fountain House
160 Dundee Street
Edinburgh
EH11 1DQ

Bibendum
Bibendum Restaurant
Michelin House
81 Fulham Road
London
SW3 6RD

Bombay Sapphire
Bacardi-Martini Ltd
West Bay Road
Southampton
SO15 1DT

British Airways London Eye
British Airways London Eye
Riverside Building
County Hall
Westminster Bridge Road
London
SE1 7PB

Burton Snowboards
Burton Sportartikel GmbH
Haller Strasse 111
6020 Innsbruck
Austria

Chloé
Chloé International
54/56 rue du faubourg Saint-
Honoré
75008 Paris
France

Coca-Cola
Coca-Cola Great Britain & Ireland
1 Queen Caroline Street
Hammersmith
London
W6 9HQ

Converse
Vertical Sports Group
Point-North
Longwood Road
Paddock
Huddersfield
HD3 4EY

Courvoisier Cognac
Allied Domecq Wine & Spirits
UK Ltd
Prewetts Mill
Worthing Road
Horsham
Sussex
RH12 1ST

Dazed & Confused
Dazed & Confused
112-116 Old Street
London
EC1V 9BG

Denon
Hayden Laboratories Ltd
Hayden House
Chiltern Hill
Chalfont St Peter
Buckinghamshire
SL9 9UG

Diesel
Diesel London Ltd
55 Argyle Street
London
WC1H 8EE

DKNY
Donna Karan International
240 West 40th Street
New York
NY 10018
USA

Dom Pérignon
Moët Hennessy UK
13 Grosvenor Crescent
London
SW1X 7EE

Ducati
Ducati UK Ltd
Avebury House
201-249 Avebury Boulevard
Milton Keynes
MK9 1AU

Gaggia
Gaggia UK Ltd
Crown House
Mile Cross Road
Halifax
HX1 4HN

**Goldsmiths College,
University of London**
Goldsmiths College,
University of London
Lewisham Way
New Cross
London
SE14 6NW

H&M
H&M Head Office
Holden House
57 Rathbone Place
London
W1T 1HE

Hakkasan
Hakkasan Ltd
6th Floor
Moray House
23-31 Great Titchfield Street
London
W1W 7PA

Home House
Home House Ltd
20 Portman Square
London
W1H 6LN

Jaguar Cars
Jaguar Cars Ltd
Browns Lane
Allesley
Coventry
CV5 9DR

Kangol
Kangol Ltd
75 Maltings Place
Sarsons Vinegar Brewery
169 Tower Bridge Road
London
SE1 3LJ

Kurt Geiger
Kurt Geiger Ltd
75 Bermondsey Street
London
SE1 3XF

Lambretta
Lambretta Clothing Ltd
95 Manor Farm Road
Alperton
Middlesex
HA0 1BN

Land Rover
Land Rover
Banbury Road
Lighthorne
Warwick
CV35 0RR

Lavazza
Lavazza Coffee UK Ltd
4 Dukes Gate
Acton Lane
Chiswick
London
W4 5DX

Manumission
Manumission Europa
C/Agapito Llobet, 7
4 – 4
07800
Ibiza
Spain

Matthew Williamson
Matthew Williamson
37 Percy Street
London
W1T 2DJ

Moët & Chandon
Moët Hennessy UK
13 Grosvenor Crescent
London
SW1X 7EE

Morgan
Morgan Motor Company
Pickersleigh Road
Malvern Link
Worcestershire
WR14 2LL

MTV
MTV Networks UK & Ireland
17-29 Hawley Crescent
London
NW1 8TT

Muji
Ryohin Keikaku Europe Ltd
167-169 Great Portland Street
London
W1W 5PF

Oakley
Oakley UK Ltd
Icon House
Icknield Way
Letchworth
Hertfordshire
SG6 1GD

Proud Galleries
Proud Galleries Ltd
5 Buckingham Street
Off The Strand
London
WC2N 6BP

Puma
Puma United Kingdom Ltd
Challenge Court
Barnett Wood Lane
Leatherhead
Surrey
KT22 7LW

RAYMOND WEIL
SWICO
Meadway
Haslemere
Surrey
GU27 1NN

Red Stripe
Charles Wells Ltd
Havelock Street
Bedford
MK40 4LU

Ruby & Millie
The Boots Company plc
Strategic Marketing Unit
Building D98
Thane Road
Nottingham
NG90 2JF

Saab
Saab GB Ltd
Globe Park
Marlow
Buckinghamshire
SL7 2JU

Scalextric
Hornby Hobbies Ltd
Westwood
Margate
Kent
CT9 4JX

SCRABBLE®
Mattel UK Ltd
Mattel House
Vanwall Business Park
Vanwall Road
Maidenhead
Berkshire
SL6 4UB

Selfridges
Selfridges & Co
400 Oxford Street
London
W1A 1AB

Shiseido
Shiseido UK Co Ltd
Gillingham House
Gillingham Street
London
SW1V 1HU

smart
DaimlerChrysler UK Ltd
Tongwell
Milton Keynes
MK15 8BA

Smiths of Smithfield
Smiths of Smithfield
67-77 Charterhouse Street
London
EC1M 6HT

Sony
Sony United Kingdom Ltd
The Heights
Brooklands
Weybridge
Surrey
KT13 0XW

Tate
Tate
Millbank
London
SW1P 4RG

Teatro
Teatro Club & Restaurant Ltd
93-107 Shaftesbury Avenue
London
W1D 5DY

Topshop
Arcadia Group Ltd
Colegrave House
70 Berners Street
London
W1T 3NL

Vespa
Piaggio Ltd
1 Boundary Row
London
SE1 8HP

Vitra
Vitra
30 Clerkenwell Road
London
EC1M 5PG

**Volkswagen
New Beetle Cabriolet**
Volkswagen UK Ltd
Yeomans Drive
Blakelands
Milton Keynes
MK14 5AN

wagamama
wagamama Ltd
23-25 Eastcastle Street
London
W1W 8DF

Xbox
Microsoft Ltd
Thames Valley Park
Reading
Berkshire
RG6 1WG